A Dublin Memoir

with the
Chicken Choker

and
The Glimmer Man

by
Vincent Flood

By the same author
The Last Corporation Man.

Bobdog Publications

Published in 2000 by

Bobdog Publications. Tel: 01 842 0229

A CIP record is available from the British Library.

ISBN 0-9532882-1-8

Typeset by Artwerk
Printed by ColourBooks Ltd.,
Baldoyle Industrial Estate,
Dublin 13,
Ireland.

Cover photograph by Vincent Flood

To My Parents

I wish to acknowledge the help and support I received in the preparation and publication of this book., particularly the following:

Marie Sheridan.

Dr. R.V. Flood.

John Fitzgerald

North East Access Radio Committee.

also Ciaran Murray.

CONTENTS

His Gran McHugh.

CHAPTER 1

His Gran

TO celebrate his birthday, he was going to the pictures with his gran, something he was really looking forward to. The pictures were always great, but going with his gran was special. They were great pals, she brought him everywhere with her, him being the first grandchild and also her favourite, she bestowed on him privileges, not available to his sister or brother.

Saying goodbye to his mother and dressed in his Sunday best, they headed off down the road, him a small boy in short pants, his gran a tall, elegant lady wearing a long black overcoat, matching gloves, a scarf over her shoulders and a wide brimmed hat, held in place by a pearl-tipped hat pin. A formidable looking lady, the large hat gave her an air of importance.

He lived with his parents and grand-parents, so he got to see his gran everyday. As his granda was at work, he did not see much of him, except in the evenings. Sometimes he could hear his gran as she talked to herself in her room, mostly about when she was a young girl. Other times she went away to hospital for a few months, as his mother would say, for a little' rest'. He thought this very strange, his gran was a great walker, why she often walked into town and back without being tired.

Down the Malahide Road, the mysterious Casino on one side, a place no one dared go near, it was said to be haunted by ghosts of the past. Why there was even a 'secret tunnel' that led to the sea in Clontarf. On the other side of the road was the golf links, where himself and his pals when coming from school would jeer those playing golf, secure in the knowledge that the wire fence designed to keep them worked both ways.

It would have been easier and quicker to have taken the bus, but as his gran always said 'going by train was the only civilised way to travel'. For him the, the train was an adventure, no two journeys were ever the same, unlike the bus, that was always crowded and noisy. A short cut by way of Copeland Grove brought them to the station on Howth Road, up the long steps and on to the platform. A small station with many framed pictures, places of interest to visit, by train of course. More important, from his point of view, it had a machine for dispensing chocolate bars, naturally, his gran would oblige.

The distance sound of a whistle, heralded the approach of a train, when it came into view, it was like a great steel dragon, belching clouds of steam and smoke, as it thundered to a halt. He could feel the grip on his little hand tighten as the train stopped with a hiss of steam, that engulfed them. His gran disappeared from his view, giving him a fright. Her strong hand reassured him, as she pulled him close to herself. When the steam cleared, she reached down and gave him a kiss, he wished she wouldn't, well, at least not in front of the other passengers. Once on board, they settled down beside a window, that gave them a panoramic view of the many fine houses along the route.

'Gran, where was I born'?. he asked his gran.

'In the Rotunda, do you know that you are a very lucky boy'. said his gran once the train started to move.

'Why do you say that, gran?', he asked.

'Because you were born before your time', answered gran with a gentle smile.

'What do you mean, before my time', he inquired, not really sure what that meant.

'It was like this, when you were born, you arrived before you should have, and as a result, you had to have an operation when you were only a few days old'. replied gran.

'I don't remember, what happened, gran'?. he answered.

'God love you, you were only a handful,' she replied.' you were laid out on the operation table, strapped to a' holy cross', and then operated on by Dr. Collis, a real gentleman'.

'What was the matter with me, gran?'. he asked her seriously.

'You could not keep your food down', said gran, 'so they had to operate on your 'Pylorax'.

'My what?', he exclaimed. another new word.

'It's part of your stomach, you still bear the scar on your tummy', she answered gently', thanks to Dr. Collis. there is nothing wrong with your stomach now'.

'Nothing wrong with my stomach that a few sweets wouldn't cure'. he replied with a laugh.

Passing over the 'Middle Arches' on Clontarf Road he could just about see the waves as they crashed on the rocks by the sea front. By standing up on his toes, he could on the other side see Fairview Park. Years later he got to know it for it's surface when playing football as 'Iodine Park'.

'When I was young, and that wasn't yesterday', said gran, 'before it became a park, it was known as "The Sloblands"'.

'That's a funny name, gran', he replied with curiosity.

'The sea used to come right up to Fairview, till it was filled in', answered gran.

'There's the picture house gran', he cried, pointing out the window.

'Indeed it is' she replied with a smile, 'we were there only a few weeks ago'.

Only too well he remembered. His gran had been waiting outside school, he was the envy of all his class mates, when they heard he was off to the Fairview Grand. Arriving to find no queue, they walked into an almost empty cinema, giving them a choice of seats, not that it made much difference, all wooden seats are the same. The more expensive cushion seats were out of their price range.

'Do you remember' she said quietly,' you were in this cinema in your Christening robes'.

'I was', he replied, not really sure what that meant.

'The day you were Baptised, to celebrate, we all went to the pictures', she answered cheerfully.

'Was it a good film, gran?' asked.

'Grace Moore, your mother wouldn't miss it for all the world', was her reply.

'I remember the first talking picture', said Gran.

'You do?', he replied, 'but Gran, all pictures are talking pictures?'

'Not always', answered Gran. 'your Mother and I queued for over four hours to see it'.

'What was the name of the picture, Gran?' he inquired.

'The 'Singing Fool'. came the reply. 'The year was 1929, in the "Capitol Cinema" and it starred Al Jolson'.

'Never heard of him, what was he like', he asked.

'Marvellous, everyone cried when he sang 'Sonny Boy', remembered Gran.

He was happy not to remember, he hated singing pictures, much preferred cowboys or war films.

Seated in front of them was a family, father, mother, and 4 children, soon to be joined by three other boys with school bags. From a large shopping bag, the mother produced sandwiches and a flask of tea. They would arrive at opening time and stay till the cinema closed. His gran said that many families went to the pictures as often as 3 times a week in winter, to keep out of the cold. By taking food with them the whole family could be in a warm place, to enjoy a meal of sorts, not like at home, where they had no heat.

He thought they were indeed very lucky, imagine going to the pictures 3 times a week, some people had all the luck.

'I must tell you about the time I got married', said gran as they relaxed and enjoyed the view.

'When was that, gran'?' he inquired.

'A long time ago, we had a great day', she said looking into the distance,' after coming out of the chapel your granda made a right fool of himoolf'.

'What did he do gran?' he asked, curious to know.

'There was a crowd of children gathered outside on the street, waiting'. replied gran.

' What were they waiting for, gran'?. he said.

'It was the custom in those days for the groom to grush* money, a sort of good luck charm'. answered gran.

'That was a great idea, gran'?. said a surprised boy.

'A great idea my hat, instead of grushing coppers that he had in one pocket, your granda grushed the silver he had in his other pocket', cried gran, shaking her head.

'You mean he threw away half-crowns and two bobs, he must have been rich', said an astonished boy.

'Far from it, we were on tea and bread for a week afterwards', said gran with a laugh.

'Did you get any, gran?' he asked innocently.

'No, certainly not, but some of the guests nearly got trampled to death in the rush', replied gran.

Arriving at Amiens Street station, they went down the long steps and up Talbot Street heading for O'Connell Street.

'Is it a good picture, gran'? he inquired, as they approached the Savoy Cinema.

'Of course it is', came the reply.

'What's it called'. he asked hopefully.

'The Chocolate Soldier'. she answered.

He thought that was a funny name for a film, was it a war picture, it must be, weren't there soldiers in it? Outside the cinema a queue of about 50 people had formed, no sooner had they taken their place at the end of the queue, than an accordion player appeared like magic to entertain the waiting queue. He walked up and down as he played, smiling all the while, especially when a contribution was dropped into the pouch dangling from the accordion. He finished his turn, and was quickly replaced by a fiddle player who churned out Irish music, hoping no doubt to catch some loose change, before the crowd disappeared into the dark cavern of the cinema.

After purchasing the tickets and still clutching her hand, they marched down the aisle to take their seats at the front of the cinema, but not before first getting some sweets.

They had only settled in their seats when suddenly, without warning the lights went out leaving them in total darkness. Next moment the air was filled with the sound of an organ, that rose out of the ground, right in front of them, at the same time the screen was displaying the words of a popular song of the day.

Everyone joined in the singing, none more so than his gran, her voice rang out, roof high over everyone else, causing people to turn their heads in their direction. He cringed in his seat, trying to make himself smaller than he was. She ignored them all,' are we not supposed to sing?' was her reply, he prayed for the music to finish. For the next 2 hours they lived in a fantasy world, his gran enjoyed herself so much that he was infected by her enthusiasm, forgetting all about the sing-song bit. After the show they retired to a nearby cafe where his gran had some tea and biscuits, he had a large cream bun, washed down with a glass of milk. It was time to head for the train and home, for him it had been a truly memorable day.

St. Mary's School Marino.

CHAPTER 2

Boxin the Fox

'COME on, let's go and play in the fields', said Ryaner, one of the gang of boys playing on the road. 'I'm fed up trying to play with a rag ball'.

'You can't play properly, it's not the same as a real football', answered Bobby, a fair- haired boy one of the best footballers on the road.

'We will have to wait for the war to end before we even get to see a real football never mind get to kick one', replied Ryaner

'I say we blow up a few frogs', said Alex, another member of the gang of 6 year old, referring to one of the more exotic games they occasionally indulged in. An unfortunate frog was caught, a straw was inserted and he was blown up, before being returned from whence he came, slightly inflated.

'Don't be stupid,' responded the bold Ryaner. 'there are no frogs this time of the year'.

Heading for the fields, someone shouted 'last one over the ditch is a sissy'. There was a charge to clear the ditch, no one wanted to be called a sissy

'You were last', said Ryaner, pointing to Billy, the smallest of the gang.

'No I wasn't, he was last', retorted Billy, referring to one of the others lying on the grass beside him.

'It was a draw,' answered the boy,' anyway, you can't have two sissies at the same time'.

Ryaner liked to think of himself as leader of the gang. His father was a taxi driver, the only car on the road, making Ryaner feel that he was more important than the others. He was certainly better dressed, he even wore 'Comms'*. something he was never allowed to forget.

'Ah, shut up the pair of you'se, stop arguing'. interrupted Sean, the quiet one of the gang, nicknamed 'Samson' for his strength, 'let' s head for the trees, there is some great climbing over there, we can keep our eyes open for the 'Brothers'.

Crouching low, they made their way along a well worn pathway, through the field of wheat or oats, 'they did not know the difference' in fear of being caught trespassing on the 'Holy Ground' the property of the' Christian Brothers'. If caught, it would certainly guarantee harsh treatment next day in school. They reached the wall of the orchard safely, still fearful of the consequences of their actions.

'Let's see who can reach the highest', suggested Alex, trying to appear brave and failing miserably.

'O.K. you go first'. was the reply he got.

Each in their turn had a go at the mark on the wall, but no matter how hard they tried, none of them could 'Pee' anywhere near the 'High Water Mark', set by the legendary 'Anchor' Farrell, leader of the big fellas gang.

'Which tree are we going to climb first?' asked Ryaner, as he eyed the grove of fine trees, standing like sentinels guarding a palace.

'Not me, it's too dangerous' replied a nervous Billy 'you might fall or worse, get caught by the "Brothers".'

'Come on Billy, there's plenty of smaller trees' said Alex, a pal of Billy. His nickname was 'Laugheners'. He swore that each morning when he woke up, his fingers were laughing, how this manifest itself he could not explain, but he was adamant, his fingers laughed.

'Hey, there's someone up that big tree, look, do you see him', shouted Alex, pointing one of his 'laughing fingers' in the direction of the highest tree.

'Where, I don't see anyone, you are seeing things' replied Ryaner sharply, as his eyes searched in vain.

'Are you lampy or what?' answered Alex quickly, 'you see, where the branch sticks out, near the top'.

'You are right, I can just about see someone with red hair' said a surprised Ryaner 'it's "Gandhi" Conway.'

'Gandhi' was one of the older boys off the road, a real devil-may-care character always up to something. One of a very large family, living in poor circumstances, hence the nick-name, his flaming red hair made him very conspicuous, an easy target for blame.

'What's up, Gandhi?' shouted Ryaner.

'I'm up, that's what's up?' came the sharp reply 'what do youse want'.

'What's going on?' inquired a not so brave Ryaner, when confronted by someone of Gandhi's stature.

'The gate of the orchard was left open and some of the gang are 'Boxin the Fox'. Gandhi shouted down. 'I'm doing look-out, in case 'Needler' comes'.

The mere mention of the name 'Needler'. was enough to send shivers through each of the boys. The dreaded 'Needler' was a farm worker employed by the 'brothers', it was firmly believed that he possessed a 'needle' gun, the thought of which was enough to create panic, even with the toughest of boys.

'Did you hear that, the orchard was left open, come on, now' s our chance' said a delighted Ryaner as he raced off in the direction of the orchard, reluctantly followed by the gang, the name 'Needler' still ringing in their ears. The orchard was the property of the Christian brother's, surrounded by a twelve foot high black stone wall, that had never been breached. It was said that the legendary 'Anchor Farrell, leader of the big fellas gang had once scaled the wall, but it was never confirmed. Now, at last, was an opportunity to partake of the forbidden fruit, fruit taken from the 'brothers'. would taste even sweeter.

A large pair of timber gates formed the only means of entrance, facing directly on to the farm yard, a small wicket door set in the gate was hanging open, invitingly. Arriving at the orchard, Ryaner and his pals stopped at the corner, trying to decide what to do, once the corner was turned, you were in a very exposed position. Once the wicket door was entered, you were at the mercy of the look-out, trapped, with one way in, one way out.

'It's going to be risky', said a nervous Alex, as he weighted up their chances,' if 'Needler' comes, it's curtains'.

'I'm going to take a chance', declared the bold Ryaner 'look at all those lovely apples and pears, just waiting to be picked, we will never get a chance like this again', as he climbed through the wicket door, leaving the others to ponder their fate.

They had heard stories of the great orchard, with trees laden down with all kinds of fruit, the stories were indeed true, it was the best orchard they had ever seen.

'I'm going to give it a try', said the quiet Dave, 'if anyone comes we'll hear "Gandhi".'

Taking their cue from Dave, they rushed the door to find that the trees nearest the gate were stripped bare of all fruit, forcing them to venture further into the orchard. The more adventurous climbed the trees, shaking the branches and sending a cascade of fruit raining down on their heads. Billy was in his element, as he harvested the fruit, stuffing it inside his much hated lumber jacket. He was forced to wear them all the time, made from hand-me-down, cast off clothes, which he detested immensely.

That same lumber-jacket was now proving to be the best means of storing the 'stolen' fruit. They were like a swarm of locusts as they systematically went about stripping each tree in it's turn, all thoughts of 'Needler' were put aside in their headlong pursuit of the illicit fruit. Apart from the apples there were trees of pears, and plums, a fruit that most of them had never, ever tasted.

'L.O.B.—L.O.B. (look out boys), came the dreaded cry, that echoed through the still morning air. Again L.O.B. sending terror into their very hearts.

Many frightened eyes turned to the gate, the only means of escape, followed by a mad, blind stampede.

All thoughts of fruit were cast aside, as they scrambled to the exit. Was it really the dreaded 'Needler' or one of the 'Brothers', which was the most feared, the needle or the leather strap? The charge to the gate was hampered by the amount of fruit being carried and as a result, someone got stuck in the wicket door, preventing anyone from escaping.

'It's "Needler" came the frantic cry, and he has the needle gun'. To think that he was so close, within shooting distance, their little hearts sank. In panic they turned away from the gates, they were trapped, what was to become of them?. They could almost feel the needles tearing their clothes and piercing their young bodies. In their panic they retreated towards the other end of the orchard, their only thoughts were to get as far as possible from their tormentor.

'Throw away the fruit', suggested someone, 'we can say we were only taking a look at the orchard,we never touched anything'.

They began to dispose of whatever fruit they had managed to acquire, hoping, no doubt to avoid punishment at the hands of the 'Needler'.

'What I have I keep', said a defiant Billy, 'there must be another way out of here'.

They arrived breathless at the far end of the orchard, all the time glancing over his shoulder, fearing the worst, only to be confronted by the one and only 'Anchor Farrell'

He was a big, strong, burly fellow with close cropped hair, giving him a real tough looking appearance. The nick-name he was lumbered with was for his strength as the anchor man in the local tug-o-war team, not a person to mess with.

'Come on, quick', he said sharply, 'there is another way out'.

'How, we havn't got a chance', cried a distraught Ryaner, 'Needler is coming'.

'Forget about him, replied "Anchor" firmly'. all you have to do is to climb the statue in the corner, on to the wall and you are safe', pointing to a very large stone statue of St. Patrick set in the corner and reaching almost to the top of the orchard wall.

'You expect me to climb a holy statue'. answered a horrified Ryaner.' it would be a mortal sin'.

Like a flash, before anyone could move, Dave who had no such inhibitions, raced foward, grabbed St. Patrick's arm, and with a 'hooch' from 'Anchor', he climbed on to St. Patrick's shoulder. A long rope had been tied around the neck of the statue, it was a simple matter to step on to the wall and shinny down the rope and away to safety, apples and all. The others quickly followed, including the not so tough Ryaner, who somehow managed to overcome his fear of sin, it was the lesser of two evils. A decade of the 'Rosary' in confession was preferable to facing 'Needler' or a 'Christian' brother armed with a leather strap.

His Gran Flood.

CHAPTER 3

His Other Gran

HE waited impatiently outside the school in Marino for his younger brother to appear.

'You are always Paddy last', he said.

'It's not my fault, the Nun made us say more prayers', replied Noel. 'you know how they are, thank God I'm finished with them this year, the Brothers are not such "Holy Joes".'

'Come on, we are going to visit our gran'.

Just as they turned the corner at the Malahide Road. they encountered a group of boys from Artane Industrial School, marching single file, like sheep through a gap, dressed in their usual dark grey uniform, knee length socks, and heavy boots, the soles of which were engraved with metal studs to prolong their life span. Leading from the front, in full clerical garb was a stern faced brother, with another one taking up the rear. The marching boys made no attempt to make contact with other children they chanced to meet along the way, with their eyes cast down, fearful of drawing attention to themselves. For their part, the boys coming from school were very much aware of what the Artane boys represented, keeping a safe distance, more out of fear than anything else, just a silent look, thankful that they were free.

Occasionally on their way home from school they would meet an old Christian Brother, Brother Ambrose, a kind, gentle person, the only brother they liked. They had learned the hard way when it came to Christian Brothers. He would stop to talk with them, mostly asking how they were getting on in school, not the kind of subject they cared to discuss, least of all with a brother. But he was such a nice old man they overcame their fear of the black cloth, before departing, he would reach deep into his pocket and produce some holy pictures, that he then distributed to each of the boys. They would have much preferred a few sweets, but out of respect for the brother, they accepted gracefully, and gave them to their mother for her prayer book.

They had over the years heard horror stories of the treatment meted out to the boys incarcerated there, years later many of the stories, in fact, proved to be only too true. Many parents in the neighbourhood when chastising their children for some misdemeanour, would use the threat of Artane* as a warning.

'It you do not behave yourself, you will end up in Artane'.

The warning was heeded, the ever presence of the dark citadel on the northern skyline cast a long shadow, a constant reminder for erring children.

Passing the shops they could not resist the temptation to stop and admire the display in Temple's window. Bull's Eyes, Peggy's leg's, Fizz bags, Bon Bons, with the war just starting, all this and much more was soon to disappear, it had already began with food rationing. Even the bread delivered by 'Dick the Baker' had taken on a darker shade of brown, their favourite white bread had become scarce, it would be many a day before it returned to the shops.

Today being Wednesday, a visit to their gran, their paternal grandmother. She lived at the end of their road, just off the Malahide Road, and this was a weekly event they looked foward to. The impressive entrance gates opened on to a tree lined avenue, leading to the large house, St.John's, where gran lived with some of her large family. She was completely different to their 'real gran' with whom they lived. Gran Flood was by contrast, a small, quiet, gentle white haired old lady, not much given to speaking, she doted on Vincent, he being the first grandchild in either family.

She had come to live with her family from their home in Clonsilla and settled close by. His grandfather lived with his aunt Lizzie in Whitehall, something he found rather strange. 'Your grandfather gets a little contrary from time to time,' was his mother's explanation. He loved going to see his gran, perhaps it was the sight of the elegant ivy covered house, with its fine granite steps leading up to the doorway, the residence, of Mr. Michael, a tall, austere, Protestant Minister in clerical dress, who must have fallen on hard times and was obliged to rent part of his house to make ends meet. His gran lived in the basement, with the entrance through a door situated beneath the granite steps, that led into a large living room, dominated by a large open fireplace. Always there were a few biscuits or fruit on offer.

'When you make your first Communion, I'm going to buy you a velvet suit', she would declare, much to his horror.

'But gran,I will be the only boy in the class in a velvet suit', he replied. He could well imagine the slagging he would receive at the hands of his class-mates.

'I have it picked out and all,' she said gently, 'only last week I put a deposit on it'.

He had on a number of occasions pleaded with his mother to try and persuade his gran not to buy a velvet suit.

'She has her heart set on it', answered his mother.

'But mammy, I'm the one who has to wear the suit', he cried in vain.

'It's only for a day, it won't kill you', trying to console him.

'I'll never live it down', he said with a resigned sigh.

He had on a number of times overheard stories of sleepwalking taking place in St. John's. almost every night. His aunt's and uncle's would wander the basement flat in the dead of night, arms outstretched, going from room to room but never colliding with each other, before returning to their respective bedrooms, completely unaware of what had transpired. He was never sure whether the house was haunted or were they just getting it up for him.

They crossed the road at the golf links and in through the cast iron gates, making sure to close them. Mr. Michael, with his well cultured accent, had, on a previous occasion, warned them about leaving the gates open. At a bend in the driveway they peeped through a gap in the hedge that separated them from the golf links, to observe some men playing golf. At that precise moment, a long, skinny man, dressed in tweed plus-fours, with matching cap, after spending some considerable time sighting the hole from four different angles, missed the putt, causing the boys to laugh out loud, much to the annoyance of the golfer, who glared at them with fire in his eyes. One of the other golfers, probably just as amused as themselves but not wishing to offend his fellow golfer, turned and made a move in their direction. The boys quickly made themselves scarce, not wishing to incur the wrath of the players.

'There's gran', he cried with delight as they ran forward in anticipation, both of them happy to see gran. She was lying stretched out on the grass verge, her head back, a strange gurgling sound coming from her open mouth.

'Gran, gran', they called in unison, throwing their school bags down, still calling her name.

'Gran must have fallen asleep waiting for us', said Noel, reaching to touch her forehead.

Her eyes were rolling in her head, out of control, a terrible moan came from her mouth that scared them both, like nothing they had ever experienced before.

'It's us, gran, we came to see you', he declared, puzzled with no response from gran.

'Is gran asleep, or what?' inquired Noel.

'I don't know, give her a shake to waken her up', he suggested.

At that very moment, gran gave a deep sigh that appeared to come from her toes, her last breath. The boys sitting on the grass verge, oblivious to what was taking place, continued talking.

'Gran must be very tired to sleep during the day', he said. 'must have been walking in her sleep last night, maybe you better go for uncle Jack'.

'Why me?' replied Noel sharply.

'I'll stay in case gran wakes up', he answered

Away went Noel as quick as he could, leaving him to attend to gran. Uncle Jack came running from the house with Noel trailing behind wondering what all the fuss was about. 'Gran was asleep on the grass' was all he said. The arrival of the ambulance, followed by their parents, aunt's, and uncle's, saw them whisked away home, unaware of what had they had just witnessed. It transpired that gran had died of suffocation, brought on by 'Goitre', in her throat and with her passing, he never did get to wear that 'Velvet' suit.

North Strand Bombing.
(courtesy of Civic Museum, Dublin, and Independent Newspapers.)

CHAPTER 4

First Confession

ON his second year in school, there was an outbreak of 'Whooping Cough', in the city, and he somehow contacted it from one of his classmates. It proved to be quite a severe dose, that necessitated him being off school for sometime. Normally, to be free from the constrains of the classroom was something to cherish. Not so this time, the dreadful, raking, persistent cough, tore through his small body, leaving him weak and ill, sending his temperature soaring. When it finally ran its course, he was quite happy to return to school, he had learned a hard lesson, that, there are some things worse than school. Unfortunately, it proved to have been even more serious, his young little sister, Joan, developed the same symptoms and in no time lay gravely ill with pneumonia. In spite of the best efforts of the medical staff in the Children's Hospital, she passed away at the tender age of 2 years. With his father working in England, unable to get home, war-time restrictions made travelling almost impossible, it was left to his mother to make the necessary arrangements. His brother and himself were too young to understand the significance of the terrible tragedy that had overtaken his family. It was a few months before his father managed to get home to pay his respects, heaven only knows how he grieved alone in war-torn England, where every night, the constant air-raids, reduced life to a lottery.

'Your granda wants you inside', called his mother, 'go and see what he wants'.

'But mammy, I have to learn my catechism for next week', he cried. 'if I fail, I won't be let make my first confession'.

'It won't take you a minute'. she answered with a resigned sigh.

He went inside to find his granda sitting by the fire, smoking his pipe.

'Ah, the right man in the right place'. said granda, putting down his pipe on the hearth, 'here take these sheets of paper and rub them together between your hands for a few minutes'.

Taking the sheets of stiff brown paper, he began rubbing them vigorously with his small hands, till the friction softened the paper, a task he performed on a regular basis, but failed to understand why. He returned them to his granda, who thanked him graciously and rising slowly from comfortable chair, he strolled to the 'Loo' *.

Shortly afterwards, there came an almighty roar, like as if someone was being strangled.

'Lilli, Lilli,' came the painful cry, 'come quickly, I'm stuck'.

'Now what's the matter with you'?. replied an exasperated mother.' as if I hadn't enough to do

After granda had been rescued from the 'Loo', it transpired that he had worn a new pair of trousers for the first time, and being accustomed to the normal buttons, he had got himself tangled up in the 'new-fangled 'zip. A tug-of-war then ensued, with much tugging and pulling, before his mother managed to extracate him from the jaws of the zip, without causing any serious or permanent damage to granda's anatomy. Red faced and looking rather sheepish, he returned to his seat, complaining bitterly that, manufactures had a nerve, installing such dangerous 'yokes' in men's trousers.

Next morning in school, with first Confession on Friday, it was catechism all the way, the Brother laying it on the line, anyone who failed the test would not be permitted to make their first Communion.

Everything was learned off by heart, like a poem, no attempt was made to explain the meaning of the catechism, perhaps they were too young to understand. Came the fateful day, and the class assembled in the school yard, before marching single file to the church. Dire warnings were posted by the Brother, death was preferable for those who failed. He sat waiting outside the Confessional, wondering would he make a mistake, forget the correct procedure that had been beaten into them for months.

He studied the drawn faces of the other boys who emerged from their ordeal, looking pale and confused from the dark hole of the confession box. He tried to remember the routine, the difference between a venial sin and a mortal sin. The Brother had been rather obscure when explaining which was which. Cursing was certainly a 'Mortaler;* taking the Lord's name in vain was another;' what about 'Cogging'* your exercise, was that a venial sin? If so, a lot of the class were in trouble. The silent door closed behind him, he was alone in the semi-darkness, staring at the crucifix above the wire grill, set in the dividing partition, the air filled with a mixture of incense and the scent of carbolic soap.

The sharp voice of the Brother was etched in his poor brain, suppose he forgot what to say, panic. Fear gripped him. If he made a mess of it, would the priest drag him from the confession box and deliver him to the waiting Brother to be suitably punished? He was raised from his deliberations by the sound of the hatch sliding open and a soft voice.

'What can I do for you, my son'?.

'Bless me my Father for I have sinned', he blurted out, 'this is my first Confession'.

'Stop', said the priest abruptly.

He froze, unable to respond, his bare knees buckled under him on the hard wooden kneeling board. What had he done wrong? The opening lines had been spoken, parrot like, word for word, better to die now than face the Brother who waited outside, leather strap at the ready. If only his father was at home, instead of working in England, still his mother was well able for any Christian Brother, she had sorted out many's the pale faced Nun in her time. A transfer to new school was another possibilty, anything, rather than face the Brother.

'Please remove your cap'. said the priest

'Oh my God', he cried to himself, in his preoccupation with getting it right, he had forgotten to take it off. Quickly it was whipped off and stuffed in his pocket, the ordeal commenced. He was out of the box in no time with only a few 'Hail Marys', and a couple of 'Our Fathers' for penance. It had not been such a terrible experience after all, considering the start he had made, his relief was total.

The gang gathered outside the church after the ordeal and compared penances. Most like himself had got off lightly. Except one, who had received two decades of the Rosary. Try as they might, he would not disclose the reason, except to state that he thought that the priest was awful and that he would never again go to him for confession.

'Come on men, let's head for the fields', cried a delighted Joey, 'its not every day we get a day off school'.

It was a happy and relieved bunch of 7 year olds that ran down Griffith Avenue on to the Malahide Road into the fields behind the O.B.I. (The O'Brien's Institute for Boy's), like a group of released prisoners, complete with jungle calls. An empty milk bottle was placed on an old stone wall and was used as a cock-shot, each one had three shots before it was smashed to pieces by a smart-alec using a catapult.

'That's cheating', they all cried. He was grabbed from behind and held over a 'cow pat', and threatened, if he ever tried that again he would be dropped in it. At the rear of the O.B.I. they had discovered hidden behind some dense bushes, an outdoor swimming pool, complete with diving board. By carefully peeking through the bushes, it was possible to observe the boys from the school swimming. How they envied them, having a private swimming pool, it was the nearest any on them had ever got to a real swimming pool.

'Come on, we better get out of here before we get caught', warned Joey. They were trespassing on holy ground, the consequences, if caught were unthinkable, one set of brother's was as bad as the other.

Joey lead the way across the field. They came to a ditch, half full with dirty water, the bank on one side was lower than the other.

'Bet I can jump that ditch', bragged Joey, with that he took a run and jump that landed him on the other side. 'Who's next?' he called from the other bank.

'Not me, it's too dangerous', said Peter, the smallest of the gang, looking at the filthy ditch, fearing for his own safety. One after the other, each in their turn had a go, and somehow managed to clear the ditch, not without a few close calls.

His turn came, and with the whole gang watching, he pulled his cap down tightly round his ears, and taking a long run, he ran as fast as he could. Sailing through the, air arms outstretched, he landed with a thud, a sharp, clear, crack was heard, followed by a cry of pain, as he slid down the into the water. There he lay, up to his knees in water, his left leg pointing in the opposite direction.

'His leg is the wrong way round', exclaimed Peter, with a look of terror on his face. They were all stunned, what had began as a day off school, had turned into a nightmare. Nobody moved, he just lay there moaning with pain, unable to drag himself out of the filthy ditch.

Help eventually arrived, an ambulance with sirens blaring, bells ringing, followed by a crowd of curious children that always chase ambulances. Gently he was taken from the ditch by the kindly Fire Brigade men, strapped to a stretcher and carried to the ambulance, his first trip in one. His mother had got a whisper that a shop in Whitehall was selling white bread, a rare treat indeed, so she had taken his father's unused bike and made the trip in the hope of getting some bread. When she returned home carrying the bread in a shopping bag hanging from the handlebars of the bike, she learned about the accident from a concerned neighbour.

She arrived at the scene breathless and insisted on accompanying him in the ambulance to Baggot Street Hospital. The broken leg was encased in 'Plaster of Paris', hung from the ceiling with weights attached and there it remained hanging for three months. When the heavy plaster was finally removed, it revealed a thin, almost wasted leg, covered with a layer of mud, that had not been washed off before the plaster had been put in place.

The bus journey home was great, even with a gammy leg, he insisted on climbing the stairs to the upper deck of the bus. Sitting in the front seat of the no.20 bus, he could hardly believe his eyes when they reached the North Strand.

A huge crater, where once there had been homes and families lay in ruins, following the bombing by German planes the previous week. The shattered remains of houses were everywhere, the few houses that remained were damaged beyond repair. Spectators gathered in the street, just staring at the devastation that had been visited upon them. It was then he remembered, while in hospital, hearing air-raid sirens going off and the sound of anti-air craft guns blasting away from the nearby Portobello Barracks. The sirens were a regular feature, every Saturday morning, 'practicing for war' his mother would say. His first instinct was to inquire about his school, only to be informed that it was safe, 'just my luck', he muttered to himself.

On the night of 31st May, 1941.German bombers dropped bombs on Dublin. The damage was immense, with 34 deaths and over 90 people wounded to say nothing of the damage to property. One bomb even dropped in the Phoenix Park, near the Dog Pond, smashing windows in Áras an Uachtaran, President Hyde's residence, and did some damage to the Zoological Gardens.

Finally, 12 weeks later, to the day, all spruced up with a new suit, shoes and naturally, a new cap, he made his first Communion. A great day was had by all, but for him with a 'gammy' leg, unable to travel, it was a financial disaster. It must have represented, one of the longest periods ever between first Confession and first Communion.

For all his life, Granda was a willing patron of the aptly named 'Refuge Pub', on the Malihide Road. His contribution to the welfare of the publican was, to say the least, considerable. Like many of his generation, they perceived the need to seek companionship outside of the home, away from the cares and worries of the harsh world in which they tried to live and rear a family. Like fateful apostles of some obscure religious cult, a visit to the pub was the equivalent of going to mass, except that attendance at mass was only once a week, not so the pub. The pub was a place of pilgrimage, to be visited as often as possible, depending on the state of ones finance. If money was scarce, which was the norm, one of the gang was sure to have a few bob, that would ensure, that at least each of the group got a drink or two. A regular feature on Saturday night, was the man selling pools, for one of the many charitable organisations that flourished at that time with the demise of the Hospital Sweepstakes, offering a chance to win a cash prize if the right numbers turned up.

Granda, along with his drinking pals, had always contributed to one of the pool's, a shilling a week was a small amount, but it helped just a cause. Each week the numbers were called out and were met with the usual reply, 'No luck this week'. The sheets were rolled up and cast aside. 'Better luck next week'. was the ever hopeful answer. Even after his retirement at the age of 76, following a accident at his work in Hanlon's, he continued to support the charity, even though his pension did not amount to much.

One Saturday night, and amid great excitement, Granda ticked off each number on his sheet and declared himself the winner of the £100.00, first prize. 'Drinks are on the house', he exclaimed, making his way to the bar. 'And the drinks are on me'. His moment had arrived. Cries of 'Good old Pop', and 'True for you', rang out, as everyone in the pub helped themselves to free drinks, courtesy of Granda.' Put it on the slate', said Granda, when questioned by the barman. That night and the following evening he had to be escorted home, he not being in a state to find his own way home. The spree continued for the remainder of the week, as he waited, in anticipation for the money to be handed over, all the while the bill for drink was mounting up.

The pool's man duly arrived and Granda, supported by his drinking pals, were there to enjoy the fruits of his successful winnings. With a flourish and a cheer that echoed through the pub, the pool's man presented Granda with the sealed envelope. Granda, with a majestic flourish, slowly opened the envelope, only to discover, to his dismay and horror, that all it contained was a single £10.00 note. 'What's this?' he inquired of the pool's man, 'a down payment?', 'No'. replied the pool's man, ten people shared the prize, ten pounds each'. 'You mean, that all I get is lousy ten quid', came Granda's shocked reply, 'I'm afraid so'. answered the pool's man, 'sorry about that'.

A hushed silence overcame the pub, they had enjoyed free drinks at granda's expense now it had all turned sour.

Quietly, the so-called pals slipped way, leaving Granda to face the barman and a bill of £60.00. to be paid from his megre old age pension. Needless to say, he was in a state of shock for a few days, the prospect of having to pay back his dept, an even greater shock was the way his so-called 'pals' had reacted to his misfortune. His position was not helped when gran got wind of what had happened, she left him in no doubt as to how she felt. 'It's an old saying, but there is no fool like an old fool'.

She repeated it, day after day, much to granda's embarrassment. The unfortunate pool's man, was given a cool reception when he put in appearance that following Saturday night, he was, unjustly, held responsible for granda's fall from grace. In spite of granda's self inflicted punishment, he eventually cleared the dept and resumed his patronage of the 'Refuge', for many years after, a little wiser, certainly the poorer for having 'won' the pool's.

For years before he was married, his father worked at the building game and he continued to do so after his marriage, that is, when work was available. The thirties in Dublin were mean, hungry times at the building, lay-off's were a way of life, constantly going from job to job, searching for a days work whenever one was lucky enough to get one. It became so bad, that it was not unknown for a Carpenter to follow, on his bike, a horse drawn lorry load of timber to a building site in the hope of getting a job.

For many, the advent of war served as a relief, the call to arms in England, where every abled bodied man was conscripted, left a void that was filled by the Irish, anxious to find employment, albeit in a war zone. His father, in the company of thousands of others, took the infamous Mail boat across the Irish sea, into the great unknown. How his mother reacted to the forced departure of her husband, leaving her to rear three boys on her own he will never know, with the money that arrived each week by telegram. Also his father's feelings, about having to leave his family behind, to seek employment in war torn England. They would have preferred to stay at home, but it was not to be. Heaven only knows what hardship they suffered, with poor accommodation, the inadequate food due to rationing, to say nothing of the loneliness they must have experienced being parted from their loved ones.

Some, like his father, avoided the dangers of drink, into which many fell, unable to cope with the situation they found themselves. Clearly he recalls his father remark, years later, 'that he found it rather odd, in spite of the severe shortage of food during the war, with tea, sugar, butter and such, so scarce, that there was never any shortage of drink'. Even those lucky enough to survive the bombing, the seeds of future health problems were sown for many, mental as well as physical. The fact that his father was fortunate to find work in Norfolk, outside London, probably spared his life, not so for many others.

He was going, reluctantly to the shops on a message for his mother and giving out guff at being asked to do so, again.

'It's always me', he grumbled.

'Well, you are the eldest', replied his mother, 'your brother is too young'.

Still grumbling to himself, he slammed the iron gate on his way out to show his annoyance. He kicked at a stone, sending it flying across the street, narrowly missing a man on a bicycle, who gave him a dirty look. Just as he passed Oak Road he saw before him a mirage that stopped him dead in his tracks.

There, standing before him, was his father. It could not be. His father was working in England and only came home once or twice a year, and this was not one of those times. His father had laid down his battered case and he was standing with his arms outstretched, welcoming him. He was swept off his feet into the air and swung around like a merry- go-round. When his feet finally touched the ground, he was still in a state of shock, breathless, and ecstatically happy, the happiest day of his short life. Not knowing what to say or do, whether to laugh or cry, he just held on to his father's big hand, fearing, perhaps that the whole thing was just an illusion and may evaporate like a puff of smoke. All thought of messages were forgotten, they could wait. Escorting his father back up the street, his feet hardly touching the footpath, he charged in the gate, that same gate he had slammed a few moments before, and ran around the side of the house and in the back door.

'What's wrong?' inquired his mother, with concern in her voice as only a mother can 'don't tell me you lost the money?'

'Nothing's wrong', he cried with joy. 'Guess what?'

'I have no time for playing guessing games'. she answered with some annoyance 'what about the message I sent you for?'.

'Dad's home', he announced.

'What on earth are you talking about'. she replied, nothing could have been further from her mind.

The tall figure of his father filled the door.

'Oh my God', said a shocked mother 'what's wrong?' she repeated, always in the back of her mind was that something must be wrong.

'Just thought I'd give you a surprise', smiled his father.

'Shock would be a better word to describe it', she answered, at the same time they embraced. In fact, it was unusual to show any kind of emotion in public, even between husband and wife, no matter how important the occasion might be, it was the first time for the children to witness such an act.

'How long are you home for?', she asked, not really wanting to know the answer.

'For a week or so', replied his father. 'we were changing from one job to another, I asked the foreman for some time off, so here I am'.

'It's wonderful to see you, but the risk of crossing the Irish sea, what with those German submarines about, anything could happen', said his mother.

'It was well worth the risk to see you and the children', he answered cheerfully, 'they are growing by the hour'.

Amid great excitement, they celebrated their father's unexpected return, none more so than his mother, she was a different person. Naturally, the boys waited to see if their father had brought anything nice for them, they were not disappointed. A few bars of chocolate and some sweets. They had not tasted chocolate for ages, it was a real treat for them. He also bought a pound of tea on the black market, at the scandalous price of a pound a pound, but with food rationing in place, a most welcome gift. There was nothing his mother liked more than a cup of 'scald',(tea). Ever since the introduction of wartime rationing, she had, like many others, been reduced to drying tea leaves for re-use, but there was only so much tea that could be squeezed from a leaf of tea. Those precious few days, in the middle of the war, were the best ever for the family, even the weather smiled on them. One of the days they enjoyed a picnic among the sand dunes in Dollymount with 'real' tea and sandwiches, a most important day in the life of the family, an all to rare occasion indeed.

It was a moment, a brief interlude, in the midst of a world gone mad, for what? A day they would remember forever, before the heartbreak of his father's return to the battle zone that was England at that time.

Rationing came into operation in June 1942, though tea had been allocated by means of a Tea Registration card in 1941. The initial two ounces of tea a week was then halved and shortly afterwards, halved again. The ending of wheat imports saw the introduction of the dark brown extraction loaf, certainly nutritious, but tasting bloody awful. The public was far from impressed but they had to like it, or lump it. Coupons were required for cigarettes and clothes, a three piece men's suit required something like forty coupons, a shirt needed about seventeen coupons. In a surreal scene, straight out of a Gilbert and Sullivan Operetta, Sean Lemass, Minister for Supplies, announced in the Dáil* that 'When the present stocks become exausted, there will be no more cocoa until the war ends'.

On the second week of their summer holidays, his mother announced to a surprised family that, 'We're getting out of here, and going to live in England'.

Her sister, May had lived in Birmingham for a number of years and with his father also living and working near London, it seemed the logical thing to do, to unite the family. With the war in Europe becoming more intensive, his grandparents were not impressed by this decision, seeing it as a dangerous place to live, especially for the children. Nevertheless, once his mother decided to do something, she was not easily persuaded to change her mind.

So everything they possessed was squeezed into two suitcases and with a sad goodbye to their grandparents, they set off on the great adventure. The well trodden route to Dun Laoghaire, that had served generations of emigrants was now open to them, not that the children were aware of what was happening to them. They commenced the journey to Dun Laoghaire with the assistance of their uncle Jack, who accompanied them as far as the Mail Boat, waving goodbye from the quay side as the Mail Boat nosed it's way into the Irish sea. The children were naturally excited with the prospect of a trip on a 'real' boat, they had no idea of where or why they were going, for them it was just another adventure. Not so for his mother; the responsibility of caring for three young children, one of them a small baby, and moving to a foreign country, to an uncertain future in war torn England, weighted heavily on her shoulders. The boarding of the Mail boat must have been a hard for her, leaving her parents and friends behind, never ever having been out of Ireland before, and cutting herself off from everything she had lived for, to try and keep her family together.

The crossing was a little rough in a boat that had seen better days, the facilities on board the ever so crowded boat, were to say the least, basic, with many passengers having to sleep on the floor. There was always in the back of peoples mind, the possibility of attack by German submarines, in spite of the fact that Ireland was neutral. Trying to move two heavy suitcases and at the same time look after three children was not easy. Fortunately, help was forthcoming from a tall man, who in spite of having a case of his own, carried the suitcases to the railway station, much to his mother's relief, she thanked him profusely. A kind railway Porter came to their assistance and with a trolley, he took them to the platform for the train to Birmingham, he even placed the cases in a carriage for them, wishing them well By this time, the children were worn out from travelling and they quickly fell asleep, leaving their mother to watch over them. On arriving at Birmingham, it was a very tired family that set foot on the platform. Somehow the suitcases were pulled and dragged from the train and layed to rest beside the waiting room.

'Your aunt May said that she would be here to meet us', said his mother, searching the station for a sign of her sister, but failed to see her. Standing, waiting, not knowing what to do, suppose Aunt May did not turn up, what were they to do in this strange land, where everyone rushed around like mad. Finally, just when it seemed that they were stranded, Aunt May arrived in a flurry of arms, hugs and kisses. When the welcome had subsided, they loaded the suitcases on to a trolley and steered it to the exit, before taking the bus to Aunt May's home.

In no time, a good meal was prepared and wolfed down by the children, who at this stage were almost asleep on their feet, to say nothing of his mother. She did not eat too much, sleep was more important. A few hours sleep did wonders for them all. His mother and Aunt May went to find accommodation, that was not too far from her home. They spent the night with Aunt May and first thing next morning they were on the move again, to a one-roomed flat on the second floor of a large house that contained a number of other flats.

The sparsely furnished flat, the floor covered with a bright coloured patterned linoleum and the bare minimum amount of furniture, plus a sink and a gas cooker. The boys were excited by their new surroundings, especially the view from the front window that overlooked the busy street below. They couldn't wait to explore the new neighbourhood. For his mother, it was not so exciting, with three children depending entirely on her, even to go to the shops, meant dressing the children and bring them with her. There was also the matter of rationing to be considered, having arrived on a Saturday, they would have to wait till Monday to get ration books from the Social Welfare Office. At home, there was a plentiful supply of fresh food and vegetables, not so in England, here the situation was critical, with a limited supply of essential food available. Much to their disappointment, they were confined to the flat, his mother could not take the chance and let them play on the street below, they became restless. The only outlet was when they went shopping with his mother and that was only once a day, hardly what they would call playing.

The plan was, just as soon as they settled in Birmingham, his father would join them and unite the family. The following morning being Sunday, they went in search of a Church. After making a few inquiries, they were directed to a Church not too far from their flat. Returning home from Mass, they were struck by the number of people out cleaning windows and painting their houses. This caused his mother a great deal of agitation.

'What sort of a God forsaken place is this, where nobody observes the Sabbath?' she cried, not that she was a very religious person, on the contrary, she was indeed a little sceptical of some of the religious practices, but she drew the line when it came to Sunday. It was considered un-Christian to even hang out clothes to dry on Sunday, as for window clearing and painting, unheard of. But she reserved her harshest critism at the sight of women in long pants.

'A right lot of 'hussies', that's what are they, women trying to be men or what?', she snorted when they returned to the flat. She was unhappy with the situation they found themselves in, isolated, with not a soul to turn too. Aunt May worked in a factory six days a week and with a family of her own to cater for, so they were on their own. The very next morning they were awakened early with the news that they were going home, immediately. (Some years later, he learned the true reason for the sudden departure. It appeared that the owner of the apartment had entered the flat and made sexual advances at his mother, who promptly ordered him out).

'But Mother, we have only been here for two days', he said, surprised with the news.

'I don't care, I've had enough of this heathen country', came the sharp reply, 'should have listened to your Gran in the first place'.

The boys did not know whether to be happy or sad, happy to be going back to their grandparents, but a little sad not having an opportunity to explore a new place, either way, they were not given a choice in the matter. It was back to the packed suitcases and on to the street in no time, on board the bus heading for the railway station, before they could catch their breath. She never even bothered to tell her own sister that they were leaving for home. The boat train was of course crowded but somehow his mother managed to find a seat, wedged between a window and the blessed suitcases.

The channel crossing was no better than the previous one, in fact it was worse, not helped by two of the W.C.s. being out of commission, forcing passengers to go in search of other means of relieving themselves. It was still a long voyage home, with many sleepy heads among the passengers and a few not so sleepy out on deck for the best part of the journey. The sight of the Wicklow mountains lifted their hearts, a view that must have inspired many a returning emigrant, and in spite of their tiredness, the family disembarked at Dun Laoghaire pier with a spring in their step. Another train journey, complete with suitcases, only this time they were going home, before the twenty bus dropped them of at the end of Donnycarney Road..

To say his Gran was surprised by their appearance at the back door, would be putting it mildly. They literally fell in the door from exhaustion, hunger and relief, a quick meal and off to bed for the children. His mother rarely ever spoke or mentioned that ill fated trip to England.

It had been a mistake, done on the spur of the moment, with no proper planning. For the children, it had been a surprise trip for them, one they hardly remembered. Not so for his mother, it had been a bitter experience, best forgotten.

Aunt Julia Lynam.

CHAPTER 05

His Aunt Julia

HE burst in the back door and threw his school bag into the corner with a vengeance.

'God bless the man who invented summer holidays', he cried with delight, 'just think of it, no more eckker'.*

His mother smiled at her son's action. It had been a long year for all of them, not helped by a cold, bitter winter. The constant battles over homework, trying to provide lunches from the small rations they were obliged operate from, coughs, colds, all the usual ailments, real or imaginary associated with children attending school.

They all needed a break, mother concluded. 'On Sunday next, both you and your brother Noel are heading for Aunt Julia's', she announced. 'for a few weeks in the country'.

This came as a surprise, he had been looking forward to spending his summer playing football and going for a few swims with his pals. Still, the country would be a complete change, they would get to see their cousins, whom they had not met for years.

Sunday morning saw them at an early mass, then back home and with the bags packed it was down to catch the 20 bus into town, over O'Connell Bridge to the bus stop on the quays. He could just about see over the wall into the Liffey as it slushed under the bridge making it's way to the sea. After what seemed an eternity, the 39 bus appeared, grinding to a halt with screaming brakes that grated the ears of all within reach. As they were about to board the bus, there arrived a young uniformed' ticket picker', looking like a miniature bus conductor, who went about his job of collecting used tickets, before depositing them in the container provided.

At long last they were on their way, up the quays as far as Blackhall Place, the Navan Road to Blanchardstown arriving at the old graveyard situated in the village of Clonsilla. By taking a short cut along the banks of the Royal canal, they saved a few miles. Passing under the railway bridge sight of roach, shoals of them, swimming in clear, slow moving water, like over-sized gold fish, really excited them.

So much so, that they could not resist the temptation to throw stones at them, hoping maybe to hit one. The fish moved smoothly to the centre of the canal, treating this foolishness with distain 'silly city boys disturbing their peace.'

Back on the road, the bags were beginning to feel their weight, changing from hand to hand helped, but still no sign of the house. He was unable to recall from previous visits the distance. A cross road appeared with various signs indicating Lucan in one direction, and Dunboyne in the other.

'We are nearly there', said his mother breathlessly, 'better rest for a few minutes'.

They needed no second urging, the bags were deposited by the side of the narrow road, no danger from traffic, horse and carts were the order of the day, the war saw to that. When they rounded a short bend in the road, the white washed piers came into view, the open yard was shrewn with an assortment of farm equipment, up turned carts with their empty shafts pointing skywards, and the inevitable, barking dog.

They were ushered into a large open room that served as both a living room and a dining room, a bright fire blazed away in the corner of the room. Aunt Julia, his gran's sister, was a large, red faced woman with a bright open face, her greying hair tied up in a bun, a rotund figure wrapped in a floral apron. She had as a young woman married an old man, who after siring a large family, promptly died, leaving her to manage the farm as best as she could, in an effort to provide for them. The hardship showed in her eyes, her hands bore the signs of hard, physical labour.

'My you have grown since I last saw you', said aunt Julia cheerfully, 'what age are youse now?'

'Noel is 8 and I am 10', he replied.

'The pair of you go and take a look around the yard', suggested aunt

Julia, 'your mother and I want to have a little chat, whatever you do, don't chase the hens, or they won't lay'.

Not waiting for a second invitation, they immediately made for the cattle sheds. The overpowering smell of manure and milk surrounded them as they carefully entered the shed, wondering what to expect. The straw felt soft underfoot as they explored each stall, taking care not to step on any of the many cow-pats dotted around the place, like land-mines waiting for unsuspected victims.

At the end stall, a small white faced calf pushed his head out between the bars for them to give him a few pats. Gingerly Noel permitted the calf to suck his fingers which he did with great enthusiasm, causing Noel to rescue his hand from the slobbery clutches of the calf before it was devoured.

'Come on and we will go and jump in the hay', he called to his brother, leading the way across the yard, scattering chickens in all directions. The barn was roofed with the sides open to the air and contained very little hay, in preparation for this year's supply of new hay.

Their mother's voice called them to the house, it was time for her to return home.' Remember now what I told you'se, don't get up to any mischief', she warned,' I'll be back in 2 weeks to bring you home'.

Goodbyes were exchanged along with more warnings to behave themselves, a few tears were shed on both sides, as they bade farewell to their mother. Before they had time to ponder her departure, from one of the fields came a horse and bogey with a hay-cock on board. They watched in fascination as the horse was reversed into the hay shed and expertly released from the traces by their cousin Brendan. The hay bogey was tilted back causing the hay-cock to gently slide on to the floor of the hay shed.

'So you have come to save the hay', said Brendan, a big, fresh faced young man.' Well tomorrow you will get your chance'.

He removed the harness from the horse and led it away to the stable, closely followed by the boys, who maintained a safe distance, afraid of the big horse. After feeding and watering the horse, Brendan removed his shirt and gave himself a good wash from a pump in the yard, he showed them how to work the handle up and down to bring up the water.

'That's a funny way to get water', said Noel. 'have you not got a tap in the house?'

'Afraid not', answered Brendan, with a smile', you are in the country now'.

They followed Brendan into the house for dinner and were soon joined by other cousins returning from the fields. The youngest cousin

Nora, a few years older than themselves, took them under her wing and became both guide and teacher during the holidays. Shortly after dinner with the sun going down, the oil lamps were lit and placed in various positions to give maximum light. Never having seen oil lamps before, they watched quietly, it gave the room a strange, rather shadowy appearance, with the light dancing on the walls and ceiling.

Bedtime came and they were each handed a lit candle, standing in a holder with a finger loop for carrying, as they made their way up the dark stairs. On reaching the landing they inquired as to the whereabouts of the bathroom, only to be told by Nora that there was none, she pointed to a chamber pot under the bed. With lights out, they snuggled together, dreaming what tomorrow might have in store for them.

Bright and early next morning, they were raised from their slumbers by the sound of water being poured into a basin housed in a table stand.

'By the time you wash yourselves, it will be time for breakfast', Nora said, drawing the curtains to show that the sun had risen in the sky.

'This water is very cold', complained Noel.

'Just give you hands and face a lick', he replied, pulling on his shirt.' hurry up, we don't want to miss anything'.

Bowls of steaming hot porridge awaited them, covered with fresh milk, the shock to discover that it was made not with sugar but salt, dampened their appetite. Putting a brave face on it, they somehow managed to eat most of it, but with great difficulty. Large slices of fresh home-made bread were washed down with milk or that's what it appeared to be, but turned out to be buttermilk, ouch. Food rationing meant shortages of such basics as tea and sugar, but having to eat porridge with salt and drink buttermilk was asking a bit much. They had become accustomed to having extra rations by not returning their father's ration books, even though he was working in England for the duration of the war.

'We are going to the fields for the day', announced Nora. 'The hay is ready and we need all the help we can get'.

The three of them set off to the hay field, Nora leading the way, she pointed out the different crops in each field, turnips, mangles, wheat and some potatoes. Climbing over a five bar gate, they came upon the hay-field, with men and horses engaged in the business of removing hay-cocks. A bogey was reversed against the butt of a hay-cock, the horse was released from the shafts, with the bogey tilted up, a rope was passed over the hay-cock. The rope connected to a rachet arm on the bogey, by pulling the arm strongly, the hay-cock slid up the sloped bogey. Great strength and skill had to be exercised to prevent the hay-cock from toppling over, the shafts were then lowered on to the horse, who was then secured in the traces. The hay was then transported to the hay shed in the yard and the exercise repeated.

On each occasion a hay-cock was hoisted on to the bogey, from beneath the stack came a variety of insects, leaping frogs and field mice that scattered in all direction, much to the amusement of the boys. Frogs they knew about, but mice were different, the only mice they ever encountered were in a trap, dead. When a hay-cock was dispatched to the yard, they were both handed a large wooden rake, and told to gather up any surplus hay left behind. This they accomplished with great enthusiasm, forming a series of small hay-cocks. For the first hour or so, it was great fun, when the rake began to feel heavy, it became work.

A round mid-day, they saw the large figure of Aunt Julia on board a returning bogey, armed with large quantities of tea and brown bread. A welcome sight for those engaged in saving the hay, work immediately ceased.

Sitting with their backs resting against the hay-cock, all thoughts of frogs and mice were forgotten, as the food was wolfed down. By evening all were tired, especially the boys, not accustomed to such continuous hard work, they were very happy to hitch a lift back to the yard. Sleep came easy that night, no time to think of shadows on the walls, they passed out on making contact with the pillow.

Thanks to some fine weather, the remainder of the week was taken up with saving the hay, to provide fodder for the farm animals during the long winter ahead.

Came Saturday and it was arranged that they would go to the pictures with Nora that evening to Lucan.

'This is more like it', they thought, farm work was O.K. but the pictures were more their cup of tea.

Shortly after dinner, they set off to walk the few miles to Lucan, arriving in plenty of time for the show. The ice cream and sweets provided by Nora were greatly appreciated by the boys, as they settled down to watch the picture, a bang-bang that they thoroughly enjoyed. The end of a perfect day, or so they thought. On leaving the cinema, they discovered that it was pitch black outside, not a street light to be seen. It was so dark that they could not see each other, even the reassuring hand of Nora could not dispel their fear of the darkness. The prospect of having to walk those eerie, dark country roads, full of strange and unfamiliar sounds from the huddled hedge-rows and ditches, caused them many heart stopping moments. The sounds of the city they knew and understood, not so in the country, where the different spooky noises put the fear of God in them.

Sunday morning, was Mass morning, the nearest church was in Dunboyne, a few miles closer than Lucan. After breakfast and wearing their Sunday best they set off with Nora on a girl's bike. One of them climbed on to the carrier, the other started walking in the same direction. After Nora had travelled a few miles or so with her passenger, he dismounted and continued walking. She then returned to collect the other passenger, who, in his turn climbed aboard and away they went. Soon the other passenger was overtaken, who waved to them in passing.

'See you soon', shouted Nora as they whizzed by. The same procedure was repeated over a number of times till they all reached Dunboyne safely, where the bike was secured to the church railings. Entering the church, they managed to avoid the collection plate at the door, they did not have any money to give.

The small church reverberated to the sound of noisy feet on the bare wooden floor, seats were at a premium. The two boys, knowing no better, marched to some empty seats at the front of the church, only to be quickly dragged away by a red faced Nora.

'You can't sit in those seats', she whispered firmly, 'they belong to rich families'.

'You mean they own the seats in the church', he replied shocked by such a thing.

'Yes', answered an embarrassed Nora, as heads began to turn and nod in their direction. Finding a hard kneeling board with no seat attached, they settled down to hear Mass. Halfway through the Mass, the Priest got up into the pulpit and proceeded to read out loud, donations received from parishioners. Beginning with the largest donor, he went through a long list, one's standing in the community was reflected on where your name appeared on that list, the poor never got a mention.

It proved to be a long, dreary ceremony with much standing up and kneeling down, before it was mercifully brought to a conclusion. Much to the relief of those present, especially the boys, more used to a shortened version of the same Mass.

They tumbled out the church doors, rubbing their poor knees, not used to such sustained punishment. It was back to the walking and riding routine, but not before Nora spent sometime talking with some of her friends outside the church. Noel being the youngest, took first turn on the bike, exchanging places reluctantly with his brother. Before they knew it, the half-moon shape of the hay-barn came into view, walking the last few yards together, they arrived in the yard tired from their exertions.

A tall figure emerged from the house, making for a bike parked near a window.

'Mary, are you going already?' inquired Nora, as they approached the house.

'Sorry, but I have to be going, I have to prepare a dinner for my brother', replied Mary, turning to face them. 'And who have we here?'

'Some city slickers, come to save the harvest', answered Nora, with a quiet smile.

The boys were transfixed at the appearance of the woman, where her nose should have been, was a void, covered by sticking plaster. Unaware of their sense of shock, Mary reached down and shook each of their hands, welcoming them to the country. Unable to respond, they just stared at the unfortunate woman's face, muttering a kind of 'thank you'. Mary mounted her bike and disappeared out the farm gate, leaving the boys in a state of shock.

'God help her', said Nora, blessing herself, 'poor Mary suffers from a cancer of the face'.

It was a sober pair of boys that went to prepare for dinner.

The afternoon was taken up attending a Gaelic football match between two local teams, who went about knocking lumps off each other, it was clear that there was no love lost between both the teams. With their cousin Brendan playing a blinder for the reds. Soccer was their game, to be even seen watching a Gaelic match, was for them almost heresy, fortunately none of their pals would ever find out, they would never live it down.

At half-time, a table serving tea, lemonade, and home-made biscuits was set up for all who wished to partake, and partake they did, especially the free lemonade. The players, no doubt, indulged in something more appropriate to their needs. It had been a long, hectic day, but the tragic face of Mary Balfe would not go away, it remained to haunt their restless sleep.

'Now that the hay is safe, we can continue with other necessary work', said aunt Julia over breakfast next morning. 'The turnips and the mangles have to be thinned while the fine weather lasts'.

This was greeted by a groan by the assembled family, it was obvious, even to the boys, that something unpleasant was in store, they were soon to find out.

Starting at the end of a drill, the surplus seedlings of turnips or mangles were removed by hand, leaving a gap of about 6" between each of the remaining plants to encourage growth. Even with each of them working two rows at a time, it was back breaking work, the drills seemed to go on for ever. To squat or kneel, made little difference, if they thought kneeling in church was bad, it was nothing compared to this. With their limited experience, they were soon trailing behind the others, even though they tried as hard as they could. Up and down they went, drill after drill, no hiding place, bent over like 'Quasimodo'. The lunch hour offered but a temporary respite, before it was back to the endless bending, they both swore never again to look at, never mind eat a turnip. For the following few days it was more of the same, if anything, the fields appeared to grow in length over night,. With the last seedlings in place, backs were straightened up, soft tender hands, now callused were tended to, as for the bent knees, would they ever be the same again?

The remainder of the week was spent about the farm yard, helping feed the animals, cleaning out stables, a big improvement on thinning turnips, that's for sure. One thing that fascinated them was the milking of cows, performed with great dexterity by Nora. She tried to teach them how to hold the cows spins and to squirt the warm milk into the bucket, to no avail. The boys were simply afraid of the cattle, and this fear transmitted itself to the animals, who reacted in an appropriate manner, by kicking over the bucket of fresh garnered milk.

Once or twice a week, aunt Julia performed the ritual business of making butter. The dreaded butter-milk was placed in the barrel shaped churn, sealed and using the handle, it was spun head over heels a number of times till it converted into butter. She would sit beside the churn just winding away, over and over it tumbled, now and then checking the transition from butter milk to butter. Everyone in the house at that time was obliged to take a turn, including the boys, it was considered 'bad luck'. otherwise. They could not help but compare this plentiful supply of butter with their own mother's pitiful butter rations. Towards the end of the week, the boys found themselves with nothing to do, so they headed for the hay-shed, climbing up one side and jumping to the lower level, joyfully landing on the soft fresh hay, like a well sprung mattress. It proved to be great fun, they jumped feet first, then tried landing on their bottoms, each jump better than the previous one.

After one particularly great jump, he felt something soft in the hay, reaching down his hand, he produced a dead baby chick, further investigation revealed 6 other dead chicks. Knowing no better, they carefully gathered the dead chicks and carried them back to show Aunt Julia. Her reaction was predictable under the circumstances, but a great shock to the boys, they were accused of deliberately killing the chicks.

Nothing could be further from the truth, they were completely unaware of the hen's nest. Before you could say 'hush to a duck' they found themselves, bags packed, on the bus for home in disgrace, no more holidays in the country for them.

His Granda McHugh.

CHAPTER 6

'The Chicken Choker'

SATURDAY was shopping day, it meant an early start for his mother and himself. 'Before the crowd arrives'. she would say. Alighting from the 20 bus in Earl Street. They crossed by the Pillar to Henry Street. First stop, Lipton's. With rationing in place, the necessary coupons were produced, one of the large shopping bags was duly filled with the basics, tea, sugar and butter, plus rashers, sausages and black pudding, no one at home liked white pudding. Many families, out of sheer necessity, used margarine in place of butter, it was cheaper. Unfortunately, the smell was a dead give-away and difficult to conceal. To be found with margarine on your bread, especially at school was to invite scorn, it was considered to be only for the poorest of the poor, those who were on 'Skinner's Street'. Through the 'Arcade', and a visit to Woolworths was next, not that there was that much on display, he often wondered to himself, just how long it would take to become sick from eating sweets, maybe when he grew up, he could afford to find out.

His mother purchased sufficient for his brother and himself, but not without first warning of the dangers to children's teeth. With the sweets safely in place, it was out on to the now crowded street to Moore Street. The noise of the dealers as they vied with each other to sell their wares, 'Apples, two a penny'. 'Get the last of the ripe pears, Mrs'. Always they went to the same woman for fruit and vegetables, her name was Lillie, the same as his mother. After the usual formalities were observed, it was down to the serious business of selecting the best that was to be had. His mother drove a hard bargain, examining each item carefully, before arriving at an agreed price that was fair to both of them.

While his mother was busy haggling with Lillie, he turned his attention to a lovely white faced donkey, standing beside them, pulling a cart load of cabbage. He reached over and stroked the donkey on its soft nose that felt like silk, the donkey purred with satisfaction at the attention being paid to him by the young boy. A sharp, angry voice called out loud, 'Leave that bloody donkey alone', a red-faced man called down from the back of the cart.

'What harm is he doing?' answered his mother just as sharply.

'Don't mind him, Missus', interjected Lillie, 'he's always the same, must have got out of the wrong side of the bed this morning, that's if he has a bed at all'.

'Come on', snapped his mother, 'the donkey has enough to contend with'.

Turning on her heel, next stop was Hanlon's. of Moore Street where his granda worked at the fish and poulterer trade, sometimes unkindly referred to as a 'Chicken Choker'. The strong flavour of fresh fish filled the open fronted shop as they entered, searching for granda. He had worked as a poulterer for many years in Hanlon's, he was as well known as a 'Begging Ass', on the street, and lived to be 93 years of age. From the back of the shop he appeared, a small, dapper, tidy man, wearing a bowler hat, glasses, with a blue and white vertical striped apron, and a wooden holster containing a variety of wicked looking knives.

The first thing that granda did was to reach down and shake his hand, leaving his fingers numb with pain. 'When you shake my hand, do you feel the thrill of honesty run through you' he would say, with a wry smile. No matter how many times they met, he always got caught. Granda would laugh with delight, and he further embarrassed him by ruffling his hair vigorously. After a few words with his mother, a large parcel of fresh fish was paid for, no doubt at the right price. Before departing, granda offered a last hand shake, that was politely, but firmly refused, he slipped a few coins into his pocket as usual.

With his hand still smarting from the encounter with granda, they called to visit a spinster sister of granda, Aunt Lil. who lived on the top floor of a tenement house in Parnell Street. With difficulty they struggled up the long winding stairs, weighted down by the shopping bags, that increased in weight with every step taken.

Lil was a small, sharp, wizened faced woman, who lived with her brother Tommy. The walls of the flat were covered with holy pictures of every discription, and as for statures, they stared their blind eyes from every corner of the room. But what really caught the eye was a real altar that covered one wall completely, painted to resemble marble, complete with Tabernacle and brass doors to match.

Uncle Tommy was a holy man, his life was dedicated to the service of the church, collecting for every known cause or charity, for Novenas, Confraternities, Missions, any time there was a religious service, Tommy was sure to be there.

'Should have been a monk', said his mother, many times. Not so with Aunt Lil, she had a more pragmatic approach to life, certainly she observed the need for religious practice, but at the same time, life goes on. His granda, having only three-quarters of an hour for lunch, dined with Lil 6 days a week, for which she was well rewarded, it would have been impossible for him to make the journey home and back in that short time. How she managed to make ends meet with so little income, and a 'holy' brother to tend for, was a miracle in itself. Still she somehow got by, what with her old age pension and whatever Tommy gave her, mostly in coin. She knew her way round the 'right ' shops in the neighbourhood.

After the visit to Aunt Lil, they crossed the road to the paper shop at the end of Dominick St. For him it was the highlight of the day, the most important part of the journey into town, all the comics of the day were on display in the shop window, the 'Wizard', the 'Hotspur', and the 'Adventure'. Each comic was carefully examined before any decision was made, he was allowed two comics a week, afterwards he would swap them at school with his classmates.

His favourite was the 'Wizard', with Wilson the wonder athlete winning many great races, 'Nipper', the poor boy who became the best bowler in the cricket world, and not forgetting 'Smith of the Lower Third', stories of boys in a Public school in England and the things they got up to, maybe his own school was not such a terrible place after all. On the way home, with his head buried in a comic, he lost himself, living the adventures and tribulations contained in the stories, his mother had to remind him, 'The the next stop is ours'.

His mother came from a fairly large family of four girls and two boys, his mother being the first born in 1907. Her mother never settled in one place for too long, constantly on the move from one place to the other. On one particular occasion, having discussed with her husband another possible move, she took it upon herself to change address without informing her husband, so when he arrived home from work that evening, only to find that his family had gone. He spent hours searching for them, it was late into the night when he did eventually find them, miles from where previous address.

The family finally settled in a new housing estate on Donnycarney Road on the north of the city, just off the Malahide Road. Over the years, his mother acted as a second mother, when her mother required medical treatment that necessitated hospitalisation for months on end. As a direct result of this situation, she never, ever, worked outside of the home even after marriage. Both of her brothers, in their time were apprenticed to the poultry trade with their father in Hanlon's of Moore Street. Jack the eldest boy, actually his 'real' name was Andrew, but for some reason known to her mother, he was always referred to as Jack. He married a widow, Dympna who had two children of her own and they had two sons. Jack worked all his life in Hanlon's, and carried on where his father had left off. Tom the second son, like his brother before him was baptised Robert, but for the same bizarre reason was always known as Tom. On finishing his apprenticeship he vowed never to work again at his trade, he had a dislike for it, probably only served his time at his father's insistence. With work so scarce in the thirties, his father figured that at least they would have a trade to work at, even if the boys did not really like it, there was very little choice for anyone in those days.

Tom headed for London as quick as he could, in due course he emigrated to Canada, before settling in California, where he worked in insurance, having never married. May the second girl was also a victim of the name change routine, she had been christened Patricia but by the same strange logic, known only to his gran, was always called May. She had worked at a variety of jobs, mostly in Polycoff's the clothing company as a machinist/cutter. She also took the Mail Boat to England making her home in Birmingham, where she married a Dublin man, Eddie Mc Carthy, and had three daughters. He was at that time in the British Army, having served in India before the war, he was discharged from the army with a leg injury sustained in Dunkirk. Eileen the next in line, worked in Rowan's the seed merchants in Westmoreland Street for a number of years, but she also moved to London, where she worked as a 'Clippie' on the buses. It was while working on the buses that she met and married an American G.I. from Illinois. Like many other girls she became a G.I. bride, and went to live in Iowa where they raised two boys and one girl. The youngest sister, Sheila, was naturally the last to leave the family home in the hungry fifties, she joined her sister in Iowa, before she to married and moved to California.

Many years later he was to discover that his baby sister who died, Joan, was also wrongly named, her birth certificate had the name Maria

Josephine on it, a legacy of his gran, perhaps?

As part of the Government's policy of self sufficiency and to increase the food supply during the so called 'Emergency', (the war years), people were urged to grow vegetables, especially in cities. Every available piece of spare land was commandeered for the growing of food. Front, back and side gardens were called into use in an effort to help the cause. Garden tools, long out of service were given a new lease of life, spades, forks, rakes, even the odd pick axe were employed to break up gardens. The call to arms was answered by many householders and it was some sight to see men in shirt sleeves vigorously attacking gardens that had heretofore carefully tended over the years, unceremoniously digging them up. There was many a sore back to be had, by men unaccustomed to such hard labour, the spirit was willing but in many cases, the body was weak. Still they tried, more out of pride than anything else. In some ways it was rather sad to see the best of manicured gardens being savaged, to be replaced by turned up sods, that had been the home for generations of worms, that were now being exposed to elements, to say nothing of the dangers from marauding birds, always on the lookout for a good meal. Life would never be the same again for them. There was much consulation over garden hedges between neighbours as to the best way to proceed, as most of the householders were city people with little or no understanding in the art of vegetable growing.

'Potatoes', said one fellow.

'No', replied another, who seemed to know what he was talking about.

'Cabbages are the best', came the response

'Are you joking, you would have cabbage coming out of your ears', retorted some one else.

'What about turnips?', inquired another voice, only for him to be over ruled.

The debate continued to the pub, with 'experts', delivering their views on the subject, in the end, each decided for themselves.

No one took to the challenge more so than his granda, who announced to all, that he was going to grow as much food as possible, something his gran greeted with a certain amount of scepticism, but at the same time, not wishing to appear negative. Their house occupied a corner site, with a large garden at both front and side, granda set about the task of digging the garden. He opted for potatoes, and so began the great adventure, with the ceremonial digging of the first sod, witnessed by all of the family who turned out to offer support. He attacked the job with great enthusiasm, after the initial assault on the garden, he ran out of steam and had to take a rest, before returning to the hard work that it was. Over the next few days the work proceeded a pace, by the end of the week, it was ready for the next stage of development, lazy beds were formed and the distasteful job of laying' fresh' manure began and the setting of potatoes. Lazy beds consisted of a bed of clay, approximately 3-0 wide, with a trench of either side to provide access, into which the seed potatoes were set, then covered with the evil smelling manure, followed by another layer of clay to protect the crop.

Each evening, after his return from work, granda would set about watering the beds, carefully scrutinising the ground and remove any offending weeds, as he waited for the first sign of a potato to appear.

Across the street from their house was an open public space field that had become a dumping ground for all sorts of litter. The big fellas on the road took it upon themselves to clear the field, with a view of making it into a football pitch. Weeks were spent filling in holes, clearing rubbish and generally making it resemble a football field. A notice appeared on the site, declaring that the field was to be divided into a series of plots for the growing of vegetables and anyone who wished to participate in the scheme to apply immediately to the Corporation. Needless to say, the big fellas were not impressed at what they perceived as a high handed action, considering that the field had been left idle for years. In spite of their protests, the field was divided into a large number of plots and issued to those who had applied, including his granda. With the same enthusiasm he set about preparing the plot and with the experience gained, he sowed a variety of different vegetables, turnips, cabbage and onions. Religiously they were watered and tended, in addition to the garden, even though he still worked a 6 day week in Hanlon's. In due course, shoots began to appear above the ground and in no time, a fine crop of vegetables was clearly visible. He was particularly proud of his onions, they seemed to grow by the hour, and became his pride and joy. Most evenings, after he had finished his garden chores, it was time for a well earned pint at the 'Refuge', pub. One evening returning from the pub, and feeling good, he decided to take a look at his plot, particularly his onions, even though it was quite dark. Crossing the street, he leaned on the iron railings that surrounded the field to admire his precious crop. He thought he detected a movement between the cabbages, but could see nothing and thinking he was seeing things, maybe he had a few drinks too many, he turned away and made for the house. Just as he was about to open the gate, he heard something fall, coming from the direction of the plots. As quietly and as quickly as he could, he returned to the railings just in time to see his next door neighbour, Mrs. Dunne. making off with a bag full of his prized onions. He was furious, and could hardly contain himself, to think that he had nearly killed himself digging and sowing vegetables, made him so mad. He waited in the shadows and watched as she made her way to the gateway of the plots and just as she was about to enter her own gate, he grabbed the bag from her hand and walked away without saying a word. It was not the loss of the few onions that hurt, if she had of asked he would have gladly shared with her, there was more than enough for both families. Following that incident, he never, ever spoke to her again.

With the situation in Europe deteriorating rapidly, another initiative was introduced by the Government in the event of air- raids or worse, an invasion, by creating a reserve emergency force, a sort of 'Dad's Army', entitled the A.R.P. (Air Raid Precaution). A voluntary organisation to act as a back up to the other services. A campaign was launched and hundreds of willing volunteers turned up to do their bit for the old sod. The idea was to train people in each community what to do in case the worse came to the worst. Suitably equipped with steel helmet that carried the A.R.P. sign and a 'Sam Brown' type belt, they called to each house in their designated area to record the number of residents in each house, including children. Their local A.R.P. man was a Mr. Hughes, a carpenter from Hazel Road, who informed them that each member of the family was to receive a gas mask. The children were excited to learn about the gas masks, to them, it was just another game to play. The masks duly arrived in neat cardboard boxes with their name inscribed on it. With mounting expectation, the masks were tried on and the necessary adjustments made, the children marched around the house, gas masks in place, playing soldiers, throwing imaginary bombs at each other. In no time, the window of the mask fogged up, and breathing became difficult, before long the gas masks were discarded, returned to there boxes and left in the bottom of the wardrobe, thankfully never to be used. It was a passing incident, an idea of how close we came to being dragged into the 2nd. world war and it's tragic consequences.

Aunt Kate O'Brien

CHAPTER 7

His Aunt Kate

'IT you don't hurry up, we'll miss the bus', cried his mother, as she exhorted himself and his two brothers to get a move on. They had spent most of the morning preparing for the annual pilgrimage, a visit to their Aunt Kate, another one of his gran's sisters who lived in a place in Wicklow, with the unusual name of 'Red Gap', an appropriate name for his eccentric aunt. Each Autumn, when the blackberries were at their best, an expedition was organised to harvest the fruit of the fields. The blackberries in 'Red Gap' were the finest in the land, or so they believed, with the hedges laden down with 'Blackers'.

After taking the bus into town, they crossed to Eden Quay, and waited for the bus to Wicklow. Once on board they discussed, among other things, just how many blackberries they needed to have a plentiful supply of jam for the winter. They each carried with them a few jam jars, that they hoped to fill, especially when it came to sandwiches for school lunches. Arriving at the terminus in Rathcoole, they were faced with a long uphill climb to the cottage in 'Red Gap'. His mother had wisely sent a letter advising of their impending visit.

Kate loved to get a letter, as a young woman living at home, she rarely received any letters, so she hit on the bright idea of writing to herself. Each week, without fail, a letter arrived addressed to her, taking ꜜ

the letter, she pretended to read it's contents to herself. The family's suspicions were confirmed when, by chance, one of the 'letters'. fell into the hands of her brother. On learning of this strange practice, they discreetly ignored it, hoping, no doubt, that it would pass.

'Mammy, is it much further?' he asked, having forgotten just how far to Aunt Kate's house.

'It's around the next corner', she replied, 'won't be long'.

'There's the house', cried his brother, pointing to a small, two-roomed cottage, with a galvanised roof, and painted red, naturally.

His father often told the story, of when he was a young man, a group of his pals and himself were sitting on the wall of the hump-backed bridge near Clonsilla. Along the road, on an upstairs bike, came the redoubtable Kate. As she approached the bridge, she dismounted, preferring to walk the steep incline of the bridge. Unfortunately for her, something snapped, as she dismounted and to everyone's shock and horror, her knickers dropped to her ankles. There was a moment stunned silence, like waiting for a thunder clap after a flash of lighting Kate never batted an eye, completely ignoring their presence, she 'stooped to conquer', picking up the offending article. Placing it in the basket on the bike, she remounted, and with her head held high, staring straight ahead, she rode into the sunset. She could hear the hoots of laughter ringing in her ears, but choose to pay no attention, when they finally caught their breath, she was well out of sight.

As they neared the cottage, even before they opened the gate, the familiar shrill cry rang out. 'Ah-ah-ah...' She appeared through the half-door to welcome them. A small, round faced woman, with rosy red cheeks, the ruddy complexion of one who had spent much time outdoors. Her grey hair was pulled behind her head and tied in a bun, as was the fashion of the day. Her ample frame was shrouded in a flowery apron, tied in the middle like a sack of potatoes, 'Wellington' boots, at least four sizes too large, completed the picture.

Each in their turn received the customary bear-hug. He waited last, in the vain hope he might be spared but to no avail. Her strong arms encircled him, squeezing every last ounce of breath from his small lungs, leaving him gasping for air, like someone drowning. They were ushered into the semi-darkness of the living-room with its strong smell of turf-burning in the air. As their eyes adjusted to the half-light, sitting by the fire, smoking his pipe was Uncle Mick, a kind, gentle person who always wore a hat, even in the house. They had married late in life, like many others, mostly for companionship and to help each other in their failing years.

The hanging kettle was a permanent feature on the ever burning turf fire, tea was served in no time. With there only being four chairs, the boys stood as his mother helped to set the table. Getting the delph from the dresser was, to say the least, a hazardous affair. Great care had to be exercised in removing some of the plates' most of which were as old as Aunt Kate, and just as cracked. His mother carefully selected the most likely plates, not before she had a few narrow escapes when they parted company, leaving her with a half plate in each hand. Aunt Kate produced her speciality, home-made brown bread, from previous encounters, something they viewed with horror. It had a strange, peculiar green colour, they referred to it as tweed bread, with a liberal supply of soda lumps, in place of raisins and it tasted awful, a small price to pay for blackberries?

She sat there with a benevolent smile on her face, watching as they forced themselves to eat the 'green', bread, oblivious to their suffering. Reaching out, she would pat each of them on the head, leaving her hand to linger on a shoulder, expressing her love of children, perhaps for the children she never had herself. He was surprised to see her wipe a tear from her eye, grown -up's don't cry. The time arrived to start picking the blackberries, something they took to with great relish. The bushes were indeed laden down with a fine crop of 'blackers', with enough to satisfy their needs, as well as filling the jam jars.

It was with great reluctance and a little sorrow, when the time came for them to leave, it had exceeded all their expectations. Before leaving, they were treated to more of the 'brown' bread and tea, plus, some beautiful white turnips from the garden, when eaten raw, they tasting like fresh milk.

He can still hear her shrill voice, as she bade then farewell, standing there, waving goodbye, till they were out of sight. They had few creature comforts, no electric power or gas, old people in the twilight of their years, quite content to go about their daily tasks, their day perhaps brightened by the visit of children. Two, simple, harmless people, who never harmed a soul in their lives, in a world that no longer exists. They never did get back to see aunt Kate again, she passed away a few years later. Lord rest her soul.

St. Canices National School.

CHAPTER 8

Moving House

THERE came the time when we were obliged to move house, what with three growing children, aunts uncles and grandparents, the house became sort of crowded. Every stitch of furniture was loaded on to a horse drawn cart and headed for town to rendezvous with his mother at the new address in Gardiner Place. They had left some time before by bus, to prepare the new room, that was to be their new home. It was to be a great adventure. Not so for his mother, with his father working in England, she was both mother and father to the boys, a role she undertook with great strength and courage. He was impressed with his first view of the Georgian house, a set of granite steps rising to a fine hall door, that had seen better days. Their room was situated on the ground floor, through a long, dark and smelly corridor to the rear, overlooking a rather unkempt garden, with numerous clothes lines, sagging under the weight of wet clothes. A very large room with a high ceiling, the ancient fireplace dominated one side of the room, a gas cooker occupied the place between the two large windows, a stale dry smell completed the picture. With much pulling and dragging, the furniture and effects were bundled into the room, confusion was the order of the day. Eventually, everything was set in place, beds were made, the table and chairs placed in the centre of the room, they helped as best as they could, but most of the real work was done by his mother.

The following morning, his brother Noel and himself were marched down to Gardiner Street to be enrolled in Marlboro Street School, his younger brother had not yet started school. A lay teachers school, with no 'Christian' Brothers, was a pleasant surprise for him. It took some time for him to adjust to the new surroundings, after school and week-ends they explored the many back streets and a warren of laneways through the archway beside their home. It contained many yards that housed, an evil smelling pig sty, a turf depot, a few clothes factories, by far the most interesting to them was a blacksmith's forge, serving the many horses that worked the city. For city kids, it was fascinating to watch the blacksmith making horse shoes, the steady beat of the hammer on the anvil, the paring of the horse's hoofs, for them it was like a fairytale. Sparks filled the place, the pungent smell when the hot metal shoe was pressed on to the hoof, then secured in place with long nails, filled them with both fear and admiration.

The other tenants were many and varied, one particular woman who lived on the second floor, scared them to death, the unfortunate woman suffered with some form facial paralysis. To encounter her coming out of the dark hall way with her head held right back, her mouth wide open, a distorted expression on her face, was something never to be forgotten.

At night, some of the sounds that passed through the house, of people coming and going at all hours, sometimes made for sleepless nights,. His mother coped as best she could. They were never aware of her true feelings, trying to rear three boys on her own, was not easy. For the first time in their short lives 'attending school, they enjoyed a 'Brother', free school, the lay teacher's were far nicer, less inclined to resort to the strap. In spite of their ease at school, one fine morning, God only knows why, they decided to 'mitch'* from school. Nearby in Hill Street. there was a concrete air-raid shelter that had been erected in case the war in Europe spread to Ireland, with no windows and doors open at each end. Inside it was pitch black, a safe place to hide their school bags.

With the bags hidden away, they made their way to the city centre, window shopping, not that there was much on display, still the feel of freedom was great. They had the day to themselves, nobody bothered them, as they explored the city at their leisure, culminating with having our lunch in St. Stephens Green, and feeding the ducks with the left over crusts It was time to put in an appearance at home, full of satisfaction, after a day to remember, they went to retrieve their school bags from the air-raid shelter, only to discover that they were missing, stolen. Frantic searching in the darkness, falling over concrete blocks, and other indescribable things, failed to locate the bags, boy, were they in deep trouble!

There was only one thing for it, go straight home, confess, and take the consequences. Their mother was less than pleased at their stupid action, they were threatened with all sorts of punishment, no more comics or cinema for the foreseeable future. The real punishment came next morning, when they were frog marched to St. Canice's Christian Brothers school on the 'Norrier'*, (north circular road), with new school bags that they really could not afford. It was a hard lesson they had learned, there was to be no reprieve, it was to be 'Christian' Brothers for their remaining years at Primary school.

One day, shortly after joining the new school, they emerged from class, relieved to be free, on to the North Circular Road, to be met by a herd of cattle being forced marched from the Cattle Market near the Phoenix Park to the cattle boats in the North Wall for export to England. It was terrifying sight for city children to be confronted with live cattle trying to make their way through the traffic, it was like something out of a cowboy picture, only for real. The cattle drovers who accompanied them wielded black thorn sticks that they used to control the cattle. Some of the methods employed were, to say the least, savage, sometimes resulting in some of the animals finishing up on their knees. The children witnessed terrible, in-human cruelty being inflicted on the poor unfortunate dumb animals. Older residents on the street, ever concerned for their own safety, recoiled in fear at this situation, a weekly occurrence as it turned out. At least the children could run for their lives if some poor animal, scared out of its wits, decided to take off on its own, only to be beaten back into line by one of the surly drovers. What effect the in-human punishment on the poor dumb animals on the public streets would have on the children no one knows, but it was not a pretty sight. The filthy state of the footpaths and the street after the frightened cattle had passed, left many wondering about the health hazard to the general public. This shameful practice continued for a another 20 years.

On a regular basis, his brother and himself went to the pictures, mostly to the Saturday afternoon matinee in the Rotunda Cinema in Parnell Street. Their previous experience had been to the Fairview Cinema and the Strand Cinema, occasionally with their mother to a centre city cinema. Nothing they had witnessed before prepared them for the Rotunda. For a start, the so-called queue outside, was a free for all affair, with no order whatsoever, everyone for himself, the uniformed attendant simply ignored the chaos. After fighting their way to the ticket kiosk, instead of the normal cardboard ticket, they were given two metal discs that came rattling down a chute beside the cash desk. The metal discs were handed to the attendant, he in turn placed them on to a wire frame for re-use. On entering the picture house, one of the first things they noticed was the size and shape of the auditorium, it was circular in form. The other more immediate concern, was the noise level. Every child in the city appeared to be crammed into seats and were screaming at the top of their young voices. The whole place seemed to be in total pandemonium, with children climbing over seats, watched by a few ushers, who paid no attention to the behaviour of the children. Somehow or other they managed to find two seats, having to fight off two other boys first.

With the sudden decent into darkness, everything changed, it quietened down to the point where they could hear the voices on the screen. First up, as always was the 'following upper'. A continuation of the previous week's serial, in which the 'chap' had been shot, only for him to reappear unmarked, to continue his pursuit of the villain. The second feature was not up to much, so a constant stream of children weaved their way in and out of the seats. This in turn, raised the ire of those trying to watch the picture, and in some cases resulted in confrontation and even fights, with fists flying in all directions. Then, and only then, did the attendants move to quell the disturbance, before it got out of hand. With flashing lights, they marched down the aisle, shining the light on the offenders, shouting for them to be quiet or else. It usually solved the problem, but sometimes, when things got nasty, anyone in the vicinity of the brawl, was unceremoniously turfed out, regardless of whether they were innocent or guilty, their protests fell on deaf ears.

Meanwhile things returned to 'normal', the audience settled down to enjoy the picture. During the more intense moments of the picture, a cry rang out from a row of seats directly below the overhanging balcony, followed by much swearing and pointing of fingers in the direction of the balcony. Later they heard that the patrons in the front seats on the balcony, a much prized seat, reluctant to visit the W.C. in desperation urinated over the balcony on to the unsuspecting patrons below, with the inevitable result. A search by the attendants, revealed nothing, just innocent faces, who expressed surprise and shock, that anyone would do such a dreadful thing. It was an experience like this that made them very careful when choosing a seat in their next visit to the Rotunda. They decided to try different picture houses in the locality, the Plaza just off Dorset Street the 'Mero' in Mary Street but one was worse than the other. Another picture house they ventured to visit was the New Electric in Talbot Street known locally as the 'Elec', situated beneath the railway bridge close to Amiens Street station. Whenever a train passed over the bridge, the noise it created, obliterated the sound of the film on view, needless to say, the patrons created their own, and not very polite sounds. Further up the street was another picture house, with the grandiose title of the 'Masterpiece'. Someone at least had sense of humour, it was anything but a Masterpiece. All those local cinemas had one thing in common, they were rough and tough, and 4p. for the matinee, about as much as most could afford, but it was an escape from the harsh reality of city life. There was one other picture house in Mary Street called 'The Volta', and he was warned by some of his pals not to go within a mile of it. By all accounts, it was a really tough place, to be avoided at all costs, it was so tough, that even 'Hard Chaws'. thought twice before going, and only went in a gang of five or more. There had to be something distinctly suspicious about a picture house that accepted two glass jam jars in place of money. It was said to have been the first picture house in Dublin and one of its first managers was an aul fella named Joyce, who wrote that 'Dirty book', Uli-Uly-Ulyesses, that was banned here!

The situation in the tenement became intolerable, almost every night there was a row of some sort, that left us locked in our room and told not to make a sound, especially if someone knocked on the door. One afternoon arriving home from school, they were delighted to learn that they were on the move again, this time to Botanic Avenue in Drumcondra. To them it sounded great, maybe a change of school, away from the Brothers. It was not to be, they stayed in the same school, walking the few miles there and back every day, the long walk was more punishment for their sins.

It turned out to be a wonderful place to grow up, the river Tolka passed at the back of their new flat, close by was Griffith Park that even had an open air swimming pool, complete with waterfall. Apart from swimming in the Tolka, they caught 'Pinkeens'*, and of all things, eels. A tricky business, that required the wearing of old boots or shoes, called 'Paddlers', and a kitchen fork. They would walk the shallow waters, fork at the ready, carefully lifting a rock that sheltered an eel, the eel would make a break for it and if they were quick, stabbed it in the head for safety. They were convinced that if the eel grabbed their finger, it would never let go, sometimes they managed to catch an odd one, but most times they were far too slippery for them.

Beside the waterfall, there was a deep, dark pool, that at certain times of the year was home to some trout. The big fellas on the road would stitch a few sacks together, they then stretched the long sack across the pool, and with a sweeping action would draw the sack through the pool and hope to catch some of the trout It was a sight to see the beautiful fresh trout dancing in the sack, as they tried to escape. It provided many a dinner for the less fortunate families or so they were told, more than likely, they were sold to the local fishmonger for a few bob.

Being good at football was a great help to them in making friends, they soon became part of the gang on the road. Griffith Park was indeed a fine park, sadly football was prohibited during day time, so they were forced to play on the road. As soon as the Park Ranger closed the gate, they were over the fence and played football till it got dark. At that time there was a plainclothes Garda in the district, nicknamed 'Leather Lips', who would sneak up the street on a lady's bike in the hope of catching them playing football. Always there was a look-out posted, just in case, till one day when they were playing 'Combo', not real football, just tapping the ball from to one another, out of nowhere 'Leather Lips', grabbed them.

Before they knew it, they found themselves in the Children's Court before Justice McCarthy along with their mother, to receive a dressing down and a fine of one shilling (5p) for their trouble. Their skill at football was not appreciated by anyone.

His mother's younger brother Tom was home from England for a short holiday, and he came to visit them, he brought with him sweets, and some different comics, and a lovely pair of shoes for his brothers birthday. Shoes were scarce and expensive, to get a new pair was really something special, his mother was so proud of her brother for being so kind. Noel for his part was like a king with his swanky new shoes, no kicking football with these shoes, he was afraid to do anything that might dirty or mark them. Not being able to play football, he was at a loose end, so he rambled the banks of the river that had become swollen after some heavy rain. He sat on the bank gazing at the water rushing by and admiring his new shoes. One of the laces had become loose, and in trying to retie the lace, the shoe slipped off his foot and into the river, disappearing below the water.

He was dumb struck, paralysed with shock and fear, his lovely new shoe, hardly a day old, gone, how was he to explain the loss to their mother. A sad, dejected figure he represented, as he limped home in his stocking feet and the shoe in his hand. Their mother was too angry to say anything, life was hard enough, and the loss of a pair of new shoes only made life more difficult for all of them.

One Saturday morning as his brother and himself made their way to confession, they bumped into one of their pals, Owen, coming out of the church, looking rather pale and confused.

'What's the matter with you?' they asked, 'you look like you have just seen a ghost'.

'It's worse than that', he replied with emotion. 'I have just been to confession with Fr. Creegan. and you know what he told me to do'.

'A few decades of the rosary as penance for your sins,' they said, surprised at Owen's demeanour, he was normally very outgoing.

'No', retorted Owen,' he told me to tell my aunt to bring some flowers for the altar'.

'You mean, he recognised you in the Confession box, that's scary', answered his brother in a shocked voice.

'Exactly, it's supposed to be secret', said a still shaken Owen.' I'm not going to him anymore', as he walked away shaking his head.

With Fr. Creegan there was always a large gathering of 'sinners'. outside his confession box, it was said of him that he was a little short in hearing and as a result, they came from far and wide hoping for an easy passage to the next life. The other priests were left sitting in their confession boxes, alone with their private thoughts, waiting, in vain, for 'sinners' to avail of their services, knowing that Fr. Creegan was getting all the business. The boys got at the end of the long queue, and in no time they were back on the street, their 'sins' forgiven by the redoubtable Fr. Creegan.

'Quick, and we can get a lift on that horse and cart', he cried to his brother, as they made their way home from school along Drumcondra Road. A low horse drawn four wheel cart was going in their direction, a chance to get a free lift home. They ran across the street, grabbed the tail-board, and hitched their feet to the rear axle, hanging suspended by their hands. The driver, who was bent forward, paid no attention to the two free passengers behind him. After a while swinging from the tail-board, their arms began to tire, forcing them to remove their feet from the axle on to the road, so they ran behind. He took a chance and climbed on to the back of the cart, sitting facing backwards, his legs dangling, and was quickly joined by his brother. They waited for a reaction from the driver, but none was forthcoming, which was unusual, as most drivers had at least a whip to take care of children scutting behind.

Just as they passed Hollybank Road. a young fella, standing on the corner shouted at the driver, 'Hey, Mister, scut* behind, lash the whip'. With no reaction from the driver, they thumbed their noses at the young fella and stuck out their tongue, making faces as well.

Approaching Botanic Avenue, it was time to get off, turning quickly, he dropped over the side of the cart, unfortunately, in so doing, the rear wheel passed over his left foot. He jumped clear on to the footpath, his foot went numb, and became painful, but thinking nothing of it he ran home.

Reaching home, it was only when he sat down that it really began to hurt. When he removed his shoe and sock to examine his foot, he discovered that his stocking was soaked in blood. His mother caught sight of the blood and demanded an explanation.

'I had an accident on the way home', he ventured cautiously.

'What kind of accident?' insisted his mother, still viewing the blood stained foot.

'The wheel of cart went over my foot', he cried, not knowing which was the worst, the pain in his foot or trying to explain to his mother what had happened.

'You were 'scutting' again' snapped his mother.' How many times have I warned you about that'.

Slowly, carefully, she removed the sock, to reveal a flattened big toe, with blood oozing from it. A basin of warm water was quickly brought into play, the toe had been burst right open and the toe-nail smashed. After it had been cleaned with disinfectant, it was bandaged with strips from an old sheet, an old sock with the toe cut off, was gently eased over the damaged foot. Likewise, an old leather shoe had its toe cap cut away with a sharp knife and loosely laced up. He hobbled down the road with his mother supporting him to the bus stop. At Binn's Bridge they got off and headed for Drumcondra Hospital on the Whitworth Road. By the time they reached the hospital, his foot was throbbing like mad, he was happy to sit down in the waiting room and wait for the Doctor. His mother spoke with the receptionist and filled in the necessary forms and was told to wait.

The white-coated Doctor breezed in the door, his stethoscope around his neck, swinging like a clock pendulum.

'Now young man, what have you been up to', he inquired cheerfully. 'playing football, no doubt?'

'No Sir', he answered nervously, intimidated by the Doctor's presence.' A lorry went over my foot'.

'Pray tell me how that happened?'. ask the Doctor, as he bent down to examine the blood stained foot.

'It was an accident, Sir', explaining what caused the accident, a little shamefaced at having to admit it.

'Serves you right', was all the sympathy he got from the Doctor.

A nurse came and stitched the toe, it was then bandaged and the shoe and stocking gently replaced.

'Well my good man, you will be off school for a few days', said the Doctor.' Just rest the foot and it will be as right as rain in no time'.

'Doctor, can I have a note for the Brother in school?' interjected his mother. 'The Brother insists on a Doctor's note'.

'Missus, you can tell the Brother to contact me and I will give him a piece of my mind', replied the Doctor sharply.

'But Doctor, he will not accept my word,' answered his mother fearful of what the Brother would do to her son.

'Missus, I too suffered at the hands of the Brothers and I would dearly love to put them in their place', at the same time handing his mother a sick note for a week. After a week sitting at home doing nothing, he returned to school, still limping, his greatest fear was to prevent someone stepping on his poor foot, alas no football for some time, hopefully a hard lesson learned.

A short cut home from school was by way of the Royal Canal that stretched from Jones's Road to Binn's bridge on Drumcondra Road, a route frequented by horse drawn canal boats laden with cargo. To see the great horses towing the canal boats as they made their way under the bridge was a sight to behold.

Himself and his brother would follow the boats, walking behind the horses, but at the same time keeping a safe distance, as they trundled along the tow path to the next stop at Binn's bridge. At Binn's Bridge, once the boat was safely between the lock gates, the horses were unharnessed and free to rest. The water slowly filled the void. When the water reached the required level, the lock gates were opened by the boatmen pushing the long arm of the gates. The horses having rested, were then harnessed up and off to the next stop and the same procedure repeated.

One afternoon his brother and himself decided to take the short cut, and with no boats in sight, they began throwing stones at a pair of nesting water hens on the other side of the canal, first having checked that no one was watching.

In their search for stones, they discovered, of all things, golfballs!. Dozens of them, like they had been dumped by someone in a great hurry, some above the water, others clearly visible below the surface. Lying on his tummy, he carefully picked up as many as he could, throwing them on to the bank, where his brother stuffed them into his school bag. When no more could be recovered from this position, he whipped off his shoes and socks and gingerly lowered himself into the cold, reedy waters edge, and with one hand firmly in the grip of his brother, he trawled the canal for golfballs. On reaching the limit of his arm and the fear of them both ending up in the canal, they gathered all that they had rescued and stored them in both their school bags.

He dried his feet as best as he could and they headed for home with the booty. It took some explaining to convince their mother that they had not stolen them. Once satisfied that they were indeed legal and her being a practical woman, the golfballs were counted, then transported to the nearest pawn shop in a large shopping bag. The manager of the pawnshop, was to say the least, very cautious when presented with such a large number of golfballs, a hundred or more, and this being the war years, it was not the sort of item usually offered to him.

'Are you sure Missus, they were not stolen?' he inquired carefully. At the same time, business is business, these golf balls could prove quite valuable, especially with the time that was in it, he knew that they would never be redeemed.

'I told you they were found in the canal, do you not believe me'?, retorted their mother sharply.

'I believe you Missus, thousands wouldn't', he replied suspiciously.

'Do you want them or don't you? Make up your mind', snapped their mother inpatiently. 'There are plenty of other pawnshops in town'.

'All right Missus, I'll take a chance, but you will have to give me some form of identification, just in case', he stated.

After some haggling over the price, and with the money safely in her purse, they were treated with a visit to the cinema and sweets, all in all, a fruitful day. About a week later, a 'Rozzer'*, arrived at their door complete with bicycle, notebook and pencil.

'Missus, I'm making inquiries about golf balls', he stated with a country accent that you could cut with a knife.

'You'se have little to do with your time, bothering people with nonsense like that', replied their mother.

After explaining how the golf balls came into their possession, the 'Rozzer' insisted that one of the boys accompany him to the spot, just to confirm their story. Without much ado, he being the eldest, agreed to go with the 'Rozzer', perched on the cross bar of the 'Rozzer's upstairs model bike. His greatest fear was that none of his pals saw him with the 'Rozzer', he would never live it down if they did. They went to the exact spot, where the remainder of the golf balls were clearly visible. The 'Rozzer' thanked him for his co-operation and advised that in future if he found anything of a similar nature to immediately report it to the 'Rozzer's, so as to avoid any misunderstanding. All the while, the pair of water hens went about their lawful business, unhindered by any nasty school boys.

His Father Patrick Flood

CHAPTER 9

Caught Mitching

'BYE mammy', they called as they fastened on their school bags and headed off to school down the road. Walking quickly in case they might be late, there was only one thing worse than being late and that was not having done your exercise. At the junction of Botanic Avenue and Drumcondra Road they encountered Ritchie McCloud, the local 'slop-man', seated at the front of his donkey and cart, on his way, collecting 'slop' to feed his pigs. They waved to him, he stopped and called them over.

'Don't tell me you'se are off to school on a lovely morning like that?' he asked.

'We have no choice', they replied

'I never went to school,' he declared. 'and I have a donkey and cart plus a few pigs.'

'It's well for you', they answered, 'where are you heading?'

'Off on my rounds' came the cheerful reply. 'First to Whitehall, then Donnycarney and home through Marino'.

'You're lucky, we have to sit in class and get belted if we make a mistake', they answered together.

'Do you'se want to come for a ride with me?' inquired the crafty Ritchie.

'We'd love to, but if we got caught, we'd be murdered', was their response.

They knew the 'slop-man' well, he collected from their house any kitchen waste, potato skins, cabbage leaves, etc. A young man in his early twenties, poorly dressed, his clothes were in keeping with the evil smelling job he had. He wore the same evil smelling 'Wellington' boots all year round, the once white inner lining had taken on a colour and a life of there own. Himself and donkey were a familiar sight going from house to house collecting 'slop'. The boys were fascinated by the gentle, passive donkey, that permitted them to pat his velvet soft head, unlike the milkman or the baker's horses that were wicked to touch. Their mother preferred if they kept away from Ritchie and his smelly cloths.

'Who's going to know? you can tell the teacher that you were sick or your granny died', said Ritchie urging them on. If he could persuade them to come, it would save him a lot of unnecessary work, the boys could do most of the collecting for him.

'It's not as easy as that', they replied 'you have to get a letter from your parents'. The prospect of a day off school certainly appealed to them, but the fear of retribution, if caught, held them back.

'Is that all? I can get you a letter any time', said the bold Ritchie, confident that he had them hooked.

'If you never went to school, how can you write?' asked Noel, logically.

'I know I can't write, but I can get one of my customers to write one for me', answered Ritchie quickly.

Still they hesitated. Just the same, if Ritchie could get them a letter, who was to know.

'Come on, you can trust me'. said the sly Ritchie. 'I have'nt got all day'.

They looked at each other, then at the donkey and cart, it all seemed so easy. Throwing caution to the wind and their school bags into the cart, they climbed on board, neither of them said anything in case it went wrong. Sitting between two foul smelling barrels used to store the 'slop', it felt great with their legs dangling over the tail board, off for the day. No sooner had they settled down than their reverie was shattered, when a familiar voice called out to them.

'And where do you pair think you are going this hour of the day?'

They froze in the seats, unable to believe their ears, right behind them, on his bike was their father. He had been home for a week to see if there was any work around, but so far he had not been successful. Not waiting to reply, the pair of them grabbed their school bags and hit the ground running, causing the cart to tilt up, bringing the shafts crashing down on the back of the unfortunate donkey, who stumbled. Ritchie, unaware of what transpired behind him, poured out a stream of obscenities that caused even the donkey to blush. Arriving late at school, they both received the customary four slaps on the hands from their respective Christian Brothers. A long restless day was endured, the prospect of going home did not appeal to either of them. It was a well chastened pair of scholars that made their reluctant way home that afternoon. A good tongue lashing from their mother, an early bed, no supper saved them from the wrath of their father, as they were asleep when he returned home. Early on Saturday morning saw them both dragged to Confession. That put the fear of God into them. The following week being holy week, and as a consequence of their abortive mitch from school, they were forced to walk the 'Seven Churches', with their mother. First stop was Corpus Christi', on Homefarm Road, to the 'Wooden Church' opposite the Botanic Gardens, followed by a visit to Iona Road church. Further down the road they paid a visit to a small private convent church belonging to an order of nuns on St. Alphonsus Road that was only open to the public once a year.

Crossing Drumcondra Road. they entered the holy ground of Clonliffe College, a Catholic Seminary, to say a few prayers for sinners like themselves and to ask for forgiveness. The long walk down Clonliffe Road brought them to Fairview Church on their pilgrimage of penance. It was a weary pair of boys that trundled up Gracepark Road on the last leg of their march to Holy Cross College. The beautiful cut stone Church, set in a vale of Cypress trees and the truly magnificent vaulted pitch pine roof with matching timber pews, made no lasting impression on the now repentant and exhausted boys.

The lesson they had learned was; if you decide to mitch from school, always remember the 11th Commandment, – don't get caught.

Confirmation Class. St. Canices Primary School.

CHAPTER 10

The Christian Brother

'In ainn an Áthair agus an Mhic agus Spíoráid Naomh Amen'
(In the name of the Father, the Son, and the Holy Ghost)

THE ritual prayers heralded the start of another school day. The Brother surveyed the 40 strong class of poorly dressed boys, secure in the knowledge that he was in complete control, both physically and psychologically. He demanded and received total submission from the boys. There was no rapport between teacher and pupils, even though he had taught this class for two years, there was an invisible barrier separating them, cultural as well as a physical; he was from the country, they were city kids.

One of the Brother's favourite tricks when teaching religion was to suddenly point at one of the boys and instruct him to stand up and recite, either the 'Lord's Prayer'. or 'The Apostles' Creed' Whether this was done to get their attention or for some other perverse reason, they never knew, it certainly focused their minds on the two well known prayers. It was not as if they did not know the said prayers, most of them could recite them in their sleep, some of them probably did. It was the fear of getting the opening two words wrong and the consequences of that error that confused the boy on the spot. The rest of the class, spared from the ordeal, held their collective breath, waiting to hear the two

58

words to be uttered. If you said the wrong one, which many of them did, it was punishment time, even worse, if you were foolish enough, having made the mistake, you only compounded it by trying to switch to the correct words, you got an extra few slaps for your trouble. If one of the boys failed the test, the Brother was too cute to ask another boy to recite the prayer.

To save himself from this unnecessary abuse, he wrote the proper procedure on the back of his religious book, just in case, and it worked. When called upon to say the prayer, he just checked the book before standing up and got it right, he had a feeling that the Brother was not too pleased with his response. The next time he was instructed to say the prayer, he again checked the book and got it right again, but the hawk-eyed brother smelt a rat. He arrived at his desk and sure enough he was caught. That got him a extra few slaps with the leather strap, it could have been worse, it could have been the stick, which hurt more.*

Another one of the classic ways the Brother had devised to inflict punishment on the boys was to give a list of tables as homework to be learned off by heart. The following morning, when the class commenced, the Brother would ask one of the boys a question, say seven times tables, but he would not ask the boy to recite the tables from the top, instead he would ask him what seven times eight was, knowing it had been learned from the top of the list. This threw the boy into total confusion, and he invariably got it wrong, and received the mandatory three slaps. Another boy, white faced with fear, was selected and same method applied, producing a similar result. As if to underline how unfair the Brother could be, he would then invite some other boy to say the tables from the beginning, which he did correctly. To add insult to injury, the Brother would announce, in a sweet quiet voice.

'Sure didn't you know the tables all the time'.

It was a familiar sight to see boys on their way to school, vigorously rubbing their fingers on a sand-cement wall, trying to remove nicotine stains. A piece of sand paper or the striking edge of a matchbox served the same purpose. Some of the smart boys even chanced putting ink on the affected fingers, to camouflage the stains, but it would take more than a few ink stains to fool the brother. For as little as a penny, even children could purchase a 'cigarette and a match' from any shop. If the brother saw the brown stains, you were assured of at least a few extra slaps for your trouble.

Latecomers trying to make it to the classroom by way of the iron staircase at the rear of the school, thinking the coast was clear, were nabbed at the first floor landing by 'Holy Willie', the head Brother, who

* The exact specification of the leather strap to be used in a Christian Brother's class-room
– 13 inches long and 1 $^1/_4$ inches wide

hid out of sight in the shadows, before pouncing on the boys. A small, stocky man in his sixties, with an angelic face that belied his true nature, was much given to prayers in the classroom, hence the nick-name. He was no better than the rest when it came to inflicting pain on children. After a 'sermon' on the value of good time keeping, he then produced the fateful leather strap and dished out the usual treatment. The unfortunate boy on reaching his classroom was given a 'second helping', by the Christian Brother, for his trouble.

As part of religious teaching, they were taught the Mass and associated Hymns through the medium of Latin. Most of the class were still struggling to comprehend Irish, and the last thing they needed was the imposition of another useless language.

Whatever the perceived benefits of learning Irish were to the class, Latin meant nothing but more trouble. Latin served no purpose whatsoever, at least Irish, when translated gave them some understanding of it's content, not so with Latin. Whether the Brother did not consider it worth his while to explain, or that he thought the class too stupid learn, they never found out. Either way it was a complete waste of time. To the class, the only reason for teaching Latin was just another excuse for the Brother to inflict more punishment, something he was rather good at. One thing for sure, it did not increase their knowledge or interest in religion. In fact, quite the reverse, they measured religion against the amount of slaps they received, as compared to other subjects.

Learning to write with a nib pen became another excuse to inflict punishment on the boys. Not just satisfied with writing words, the actual letters had to be only as the Brother decreed it should be. A broad stroke for downwards lines, and a light stroke upwards, had to be exactly as the Brother ordained, with no variation permitted. This entailed spitting in your hand, dipping the inked nib in the spit for upward strokes to keep the line light to produce the correct texture, and woe betide the one who dared to deviate. The Brother would walk between the rows of seats, leather at the ready, on the look-out for any transgressors who might defy him. It was difficult enough learning to write, what with grammar and spellings to cope with, without the constant threat of punishment hanging over their heads. Most of the boys tried their best to make a reasonable attempt at the writing, more out of fear of the consequences than for any literary achievement. They wondered why the Brother hated them so much, he never missed an opportunity to inflict punishment, after all they were only children.

One lunch time, his brother Noel arrived home in a lather of sweat, after running all the way home from school. As it so happened, his father, who was not working at that time was there.

'What has you so late?', asked his mother, who had been trying to keep the food warm.' Will you have time to eat your dinner?'

'The Brother kept us in', Noel replied. Trying to catch his breath. 'One of the lads answered back, so we all had to pay'.

'Take your time eating the dinner', said his father, 'your dinner is more important than any Christian Brother.'

'But Da, I have to be back in time or the Brother will kill me', cried a frightened Noel.

'Not to worry', answered his father firmly, he was not a man to get excited easily. 'I'll go with you, just in case'.

It was a troubled Noel who gulped down his dinner, ever fearful of what might happen at school. Sitting on the crossbar of the bike, as they headed for school, he did not know whether to be happy or sad. Glad that his father came with him, but at the same time thinking what the Brother might do when his father left. There arrival in the school yard aroused much curiosity, especially when they saw how tall his father was. To small children he looked like a giant, he was over six foot four tall!

Very few parents ever came near the school, and there was an air of anticipation as his father escorted him to the classroom, and knocked on the door. It was opened by the Brother, who stepped back when confronted by the tall figure that framed the door. His already pale face turned 'a whiter shade of pale', at the sight before him.

'My son was very late getting home from school today because you saw fit to detain the whole class', said his father calmly but firmly.' I trust that this will not happen again'.

The Brother was speechless, as he looked at the overpowering figure standing there.

'It was a misunderstanding', replied the sheep faced Brother. 'I can assure you that it will not happen again'.

'I have more important things to be doing with my time, than having to bring a frightened child to school', stated his father in no uncertain terms, looking the Brother straight in the eye. 'By the way, while I am here, I would like to speak to the head Brother'.

'I'll see if I can locate him for you', said the Brother, as he rushed away, happy to put some distance between them. He returned a few minutes later to say that the head Brother was indisposed at the moment, perhaps some other time. His father just gave the Brother a long, hard look, before departing the school, leaving the Brother to return to the classroom, not looking so tough. The boys heard later that 'Holy Willie', had been spotted coming out of the toilets when he heard that the coast was clear. In spite of Noel's fears, there were no repercussions following his father's visit. When faced with someone bigger than themselves, a bully is not so brave after all.

Not all teachers were Brothers. The previous year in 5th class, they had a lay Teacher, Master Higgins. Their hopes were high of the prospect of a class without a Christian Brother. They soon learned that there was no escape for them, they were destined to be forever at the mercy of a school system that cared little for children. Master Higgins proved to be just as severe as any Christian Brother. In fact he was worse, instead of the standard leather strap, he employed a 12" wooden stick, that hurt more. He was fanatical about Irish and he tried to teach every subject through the medium of Irish, a subject not dear to the hearts of city children. They had only began to learn Irish when starting school, there was not tradition in any of their families of speaking Irish.

Algebra, at the best of times, is a abstract subject difficult to understand, especially for 12 year olds. It takes time and patience to teach algebra in English, you can imagine trying to reason out how A+B=C in Irish. It was beyond them. As a result, much pain and suffering was endured by the boys, leaving them with an abiding dislike of the Irish language. In the course of a punishment session, one of the boys had the misfortune to withdraw his hand, making the Master miss with the stick. The Master grabbed the boy's hand by the wrist to steady the his hand and then brought the stick down hard. At the very last instant, instead of drawing his hand back for the second time, he inadvertently pushed it forward just as the stick came thundering down, causing the Master to strike himself on the back of his hand. His cry of pain as he dropped the stick, was felt by the boys. Long accustomed to the power of the stick, they were happy to see the teacher get a dose of his own medicine. The Master tucked his injured hand under his arm to ease the pain. The class watched in total silence, wanting to cheer though not daring. The boy stood transfixed, unable to move. He knew he was in serious trouble and would pay a high price for his transgression. When Master Higgins regained his composure, he signalled to the boy to return to his seat. With blazing eyes he retrieved the dreaded stick and placed it firmly on his desk. Still rubbing his sore hand that showed a deep red mark across the back, he addressed the class, in Irish, of course.

'Let this be a warning to you all, any boy who dares to pull back his hand in future, will get double the punishment, is that clear?' Not all of the boys understood what the Master said in Irish, but they got the message, loud and clear. The poor frightened boy sat in a sort of trance, waiting for the sword to fall. He expected to be severely thrashed for his behaviour. Nothing happened, leaving him in a limbo; better to get the beating over and done with. The not knowing only prolonged the agony, it filled him with apprehension for days. Each morning when he entered the classroom, he asked himself, was this to be the fateful day of reckoning, but it never happened. The psychological game was far more damaging. At the end of term, the class 'almost' welcomed the return of the Christian Brother not that they had much choice!

Each year, close to the end of the school term, a 'trainee' teacher, arrived in the class, sometimes it was a lay teacher, more often than not, a bright, shiny faced apprentice Christian Brother, not that it made much difference to the pupils, one was as mean as the other.

The Trainee Brother would address the class with a forced smile of embarrassment on his face, as he tried to win the confidence of the boys. Those boys were battle hardened veterans of many campaigns, they could see through a phoney Brother in no time. The boys saw it only as a extension of the 'real' Brother except that the Trainee did not have a leather strap. No one tried to take advantage of these novice Brothers, not with the ever presence of the real Brother at the rear of the classroom, keeping a baleful eye on them. During the course of the morning, the real Brother had occasion to leave the classroom, only then did the boys attempt to distract the trainee Brother from his task. With the return of the real Brother a short time later, the boys reverted to their normal behaviour of total submission. The 'real' Brother resumed his vigil at the rear of the classroom, silently observing.

He spotted one unfortunate boy 'cogging' sums from one of his class mates – a normal practice. Quietly, silently, he slid up behind the culprit and without warning, slapped the boy on the back of the head, sending his face crashing down on to the wooden desk.

The boy cried out with pain, his nose started to bleed, needless to say, the expression on his poor face, was one of total shock. The other boys, having learned from bitter experience, the only thing to do was to keep your head down, as if nothing had happened. The boy tried to stem the flow of blood with a handkerchief, borrowed from a classmate, he did not have one of his own.

The Brother, realising that perhaps he had for once, gone a little too far, especially in the presence of a witness, quickly escorted the distraught boy to the bathroom, where his face was washed, removing all traces of blood. With the return of the boy to the classroom, it was nervous 'trainee' Brother that tried to interest the class in, of all subjects, poetry! The real Brother just gave the class a long, hard look, as if to say' who's next?' As for the novice Brother, he appeared just as shocked as the injured boy, obviously at a loss as to what to do or say. Lunch-hour was a welcome relief for everybody, especially the 'trainee' Brother. This introduction to the real world of teaching in an inner city school was far removed from the ideals of the training college. In time he too would probably become just like the real Brother, another sadist.

The classroom was unofficially divided into different levels of pupils. The front rows were for the class swots. The middle rows were the preserve of boys who just wanted to keep their heads down and survive. The back-row boys, were just going through the motions of learning. Nothing was expected from them, so they kept quiet and did enough to keep the Brother at bay. There was one golden rule in the classroom, and that was, never ask a question. It was not encouraged by the Brother. If you asked a question, you were not paying attention, and liable to be rewarded by a few slaps. So it came as a surprise during religion class when one of the back-row boys raised his hand. For a question to come from a pupil, was to say the least, unusual, for that question to come from one of the back-row boys caused even the Brother to take note!

'Muldoon, you have a question?', inquired the Brother, the tone of his voice was acid.

'Yes, Sir', replied Muldoon, as a stillness descended on the classroom.

'And what might that question be?' said the Brother still surprised at being asked a question.

'Sir, can you explain what the words of the Hail Mary mean', he asked in all innocence and ignorance.

'What words do you not understand?', asked the Brother quietly, a little to quietly for comfort.

'The part that goes, "Blessed is the fruit of thy womb, Jesus".' He was not trying to embarrass the Brother by asking awkward questions, but like the rest of the class, they had no idea what it meant. They recited that prayer every day of their young lives but had not a clue what they were saying.

Poor Muldoon, he was not the brightest in the class, but he was not devious, in fact he was well liked by the class. Coming as he did from a very poor family, his clothes were always in a dreadful state, tread bare and worn, his shoes barely covered his feet, with newspaper 'in-soles' to keep his feet warm.

The Brothers reaction was immediate and swift. He reached for the leather strap and went for Muldoon bald-headed. He received his punishment without a murmur. Never, ever again did he ask a question in school and the same applied to the rest of the class.

Once or twice a year, the whole class was coerced into going to confession in the school. There was no question of whether one wished to go or not, the class was told that they were all going to confession –

end of story! It was not that they had any objection to going, most considered it a welcome diversion, a chance to get out of the class room for a few minutes. The problem was, that when attending confession in the school, you were confronted directly by the priest, person to person. In a normal confession box, you were in complete darkness, anonymous, with a wire grill separating you from the priest. Not so in school, the priest was seated in a chair in the school office, the pupil just knelt down on the hardwood floor beside the priest and told him your confession, literally looking him in the face. The boys found this situation very intimidating. It scared them to death being so near the Priest, telling their 'sins', not that children had many to confess. It proved to be a little to much for some of the boys, the embarrassment suffered, the fear that what you were telling might be over heard, caused them a lot of grief. Perhaps their fears were unfounded, but they were children who fervently believed in the Church and it's sacraments, it undermined their very belief of the sanctity of the confessional.

The Brother was a medium sized, fair-haired man in his early thirties, with a receding hair line, a black sutane to his feet, pulled together by a sash, a half-sized white collar encircling his strong neck. The black sutane only served to alienate the boys even more; they perceived it as a symbol of authority, like a policeman or a judge.

The almost non-existent relationship between teacher and pupils had deteriorated rapidly following an incident involving the school football team. Some weeks before there appeared in an evening paper, a photograph of 'Stella Maris' under 14 soccer team that had just won the Paddy Thunder Cup. Unfortunately, most of the team also played for the school Gaelic team that was within one match of winning the schools league. It sparked off an almighty witch-hunt by the Brother, culminating with the team's withdrawal from the school league, depriving the boys of another medal. Like all the Christian Brothers he was a G.A.A.* man and had made it abundantly clear that they would not countenance any 'foreign games'. He was singled out for special treatment by virtue of the fact that he was related to prominent Shamrock Rover's player at that time, Tommy Eglington.

The very mention of the word soccer was sufficient to provoke an outbreak of terror in the classroom. Any boy worth his salt jumped at the chance to play for his school at whatever sport, to have a winner's medal snatched from his grasp because of some stupid ban was heartbreaking. It instilled in each boy, a dislike of all things associated with the G.A.A.

It was particularly cold morning and the boys were sitting frozen in their short pants, as was the fashion of the time, waiting for the heat to come on. He was one of the few in long pants, having jumped' into 'longers'* at Christmas, even though he had to endure a lot of slagging from the other boys at the time, he was having the last laugh now.

'Exercise'*, said the Brother, in a soft gentle voice, that carried more menace than a loud command. It sent shivers through the class, especially those who had not bothered to prepare any homework.' Those who have completed their homework hand them up, and those who have not, form a queue at the back of the class'. The irony escaped them. First the prayers, then the 'Inquisition'.

If questioned by the Brother, the answer was given with no great sense of conviction, a wrong answer was suitably punished. It created an air of fear and distrust, numbing the mind, inducing a state of mental paralysis, reducing the unfortunate students to a helpless moron, with dire consequences, for him.

The Brother commenced correcting the homework, leaving the boys without homework standing at the back of the class, for what seemed an eternity pondering their fate. They tried to warm their cold hands by blowing on them, or putting them down their trousers, in preparation for the leather strap. If you are going to receive punishment, better to have warm hands.

The Brother finished correcting the homework and looked around at the class, who waited for the inevitable next stage. They all knew what to expect, what was coming.

'What is your excuse for not doing homework?' inquired the Brother softly, as if he was looking forward to the beating of children.

The first boy reluctantly stepped forward, mumbling something about his granny being sick. This excuse was dismissed by the Brother, who demanded his pound of flesh.

'Hold out your hand'. He was flexing the leather strap in anticipation.

The boys firmly believed that sewn inside the strap were coins, to make it hurt even more. It was then soaked in vinegar to keep it as stiff as possible and to inflict the maximum pain. After receiving 5 slaps he returned to his seat in great pain, tears welled in his eyes. 'Next'. Another boy moved forward and got an extra few slaps for being foolish enough to pull his hand back making the Brother miss. The look of terror on the faces of the boys as they waited their turn had to be seen to be believed. The rest of the class watched in complete silence, thankful that they had made an attempt at the homework. For most of them, it was only done to avoid punishment, not to aquire knowledge.

The last boy to step forward was McGuirk, a well built boy, tall for his age, who kept to himself. Unfortunately he was a 'Ciothóg'. (a left-handed boy). From his first day in school, he had been forced to write with his right hand, each year when he changed class, he had to go through the same process of indoctrination to the right hand. Sometimes when writing a composition he would 'chance his arm', and write with his natural left hand, but if caught he got the full treatment.

The Brother looking at him said mockingly. 'Ah, McGurk, it's you again, this is the third day in a row. We will have to make an example of you, bend down'.

'No, Sir', came the reply.

'Did I hear correctly?'

'Yes, Sir. I will take my punishment on my hands, but I will not bend down', he answered.

The look of disbelief on the face of the Brother was clearly visible. His authority had never been called into question before. His face was white with fury, his bottom lip trembled, the knuckles on his hand tightened on the leather strap, the boys had never witnessed anything like it before.

'Bend down immediately or else', instructed the Brother, trying to control himself. Again McGurk refused. The class waited, not knowing what to expect, you could cut the silence with a blunt knife.

He made a grab for the boy and they struggled for a moment in front of the astonished class. Suddenly McGurk, in trying to escape his tormentor, grabbed the sash that was around the Brother's waist, and catching him off balance, swung him across the classroom. He crashed into the blackboard and easel, bringing it down upon himself with a mighty crash, the sound of which reverberated through the whole school.

The class was frozen in their seats, unable to move, never having seen anything like it before. McGurk stood looking at the Brother lying on the floor, out cold. He turned and legged it out the door. You couldn't see his arse for dust as he ran down the corridor and out of the school. A quiet cheer was heard from the back of the class. The boys at the front remained silent, afraid to express their true feelings.

'Is he dead'?, whispered one of the boys.

'No such luck', came the quick reply, echoing many of their sentiments.

'I wouldn't like to be in McGurk's shoes when your man comes to', said another voice.

'What do you mean?' he should get a medal', was the answer he got.

'Maybe we should get some help, he's out cold'.

'Mind your own business, he had it coming', was the general consensus.

There was a movement from the Brother, he struggled to his feet, holding his head, as he tried to untangle himself from the blackboard and easel. Glaring at the stunned class, before he struggled out the door after McGurk.

No sooner had he left the class, than he was followed by a great cheer from the whole class that was heard throughout the school. For the first time in their short lives they were able to express themselves without fear of reprisal. A few minutes later the Brother-returned to the classroom, and the look on his face said it all. He slammed the door behind him and turned slowly to face the by now frightened class, they would pay dearly for their moment in the sun.

'Now we will see who will be cheering. By the time I'm finished with you lot, there won't be much to cheer about', he said with menace in his voice. 'As for McGurk, I'll deal with him later'.

They suffered that day and for the rest of the term but nothing could take away the pleasure they had experienced that day. Their class was the envy of all the school, as a result of the incident. The story was told and retold, it gained with each telling, especially the knockout, it went from one minute to fifteen minutes, it was compared to the famous 'long count' in the Dempsey - Tunney fight. As for McGurk, he never came back.

In 7th class, their last year in Primary school, whether by accident or design, they got a nice teacher, Master O' Shea. A large, soft easy going man with steel grey hair, and a great pair of bushy eyebrows.

He was so far removed from the Brothers and lay teachers they had experienced over the years that they had some difficulty adjusting to a teacher that did not hate them. For a start he did not have a leather strap to beat them, his gentle and kind ways helped restore some respect for a school system that thrived on punishment alone. The response of the class was mixed, some were so scared from the constant terror experienced from the other teaching staff, that they would carry the scars into adult life.

Others, perhaps realising that this was to be their last year in school, were able, for the first time in their short school life, actually to take education seriously, thanks to Master O'Shea's encouragement. They respected him and because he respected them none of the boys took advantage of his kindness. With the threat of punishment removed from the classroom, they learned more in that last year in school than all the other years put together, or so they believed. For most of the class, this was to be their last association with formal education, a few lucky ones went to Tech. but the majority went straight to whatever work that was available. Being semi-illiterate and with no skills, most went to low pay jobs with little chance of advancement. Not one of the class entered secondary school, no one even sat the entrance exam. The fee's saw to that, as for the scholarships available, they were hardly worth the trouble. Each family needed every penny they could earn just to survive.

With his parents and brothers

CHAPTER 11

The Glimmer Man

IT was the coldest, bitterest winter in living memory. The ornate icy patterned windows looked out on to a snow covered yard. Inside the pale remains of a turf fire lay frozen in the grate, its lingering smell filled the cold air.

His nose peeped out from beneath the warm bed covers.

'God, it's cold', he murmured to himself, reluctant to venture from the cosy warmth of the bed. 'Mammy, is it time to get up?'

'It certainly is, I'll chance turning on the gas for a few minutes', replied his mother.

'What will happen if the Glimmer-man comes', he asked, referring to the man from the gas company, whose function was to insure strict adherence of consumers to the necessary controls imposed by the shortage of gas supplies.

During the war years and after, gas was rationed and strictly controlled, with full pressure only available at certain designated times. Off peak, the pressure was reduced to a bare minimum, since some gas had to be retained in the system to prevent an air-lock. Anyone found using gas off-peak, meant instant withdrawal of gas supplies. With other fuel supplies practically non-existent, to be reduced to an open fire situation and all that implied, was piling hardship upon hardship.

His mother had spent the previous evening knitting, well into the night, something she did on a regular basis, not for pleasure but for cash. With the times that were in it, every little helped. A company in town paid so much per item, mostly knitted jumpers. He never did find out how much they paid but considering the amount of work she put into it, a lot he hoped. The wool was delivered to the house in rather oily hanks, not properly refined, a hang over from the war years. This required time spent, arms outstretched supporting the hank of wool, as his mother went through the slow process of converting it to more manageable balls of wool which for him was a tiring exercise.

Each item knitted was required to conform to a certain width and length, which in most cases necessitated much pulling and tugging by his mother to make up for any shortcomings that may have occurred in the making of the garment. Any spare wool was then knitted into socks or jumpers of various shades and colours. The jumpers were great but the socks left a lot to be desired, especially the lumpy heels.

They huddled round the gas cooker, his mother, two brothers and himself, each trying to warm their cold hands on the pathetic glimmer of gas. An electric fire was unheard of.

The knock, knock, on the door, sent shivers through each of them. They were caught, the gas would be cut off, leaving them with only the open fire to cook upon. Again, knock, knock. His mother quick as a flash turned off the gas and at the same time grabbed the wet dish cloth, and in a blaze of steam tried to cool the gas ring. The first thing the Glimmer man would do was to place his hand on the gas ring to see if it had been in use.

'I'm coming', cried his mother to the persistent knocking on the door. With much blowing and waving of hands in an attempt to disperse the steam, she slowly opened the door.

'Mrs. Daly, my God, I thought it was the Glimmer man*, said a much relieved mother.

'Sorry if I gave you a fright', replied Mrs. Daly.

'It's all right, we were trying to get some heat into the room', answered his mother. 'We are down to our last bit of turf'.

'That's why I called so early. I heard that there is a place in Dorset Street that's selling logs by the bag'.

'Where about's in Dorset Street, asked his mother, delighted to hear anything that would help the situation

'This side of Eccles Street. You know, under the arch?', came the reply. Only one problem!'

'There would be a catch in it', answered his mother with a resigned sigh. 'There always is'.

'They only give one sack to each person', said Mrs. Daly.

'Is that all?', replied a relieved mother. 'We can take the box-car and two of the boys with me'.

'Are you sure? The weather outside is appalling', answered a concerned Mrs. Daly.

For weeks it had been snowing. Everything was at a standstill, roads were blocked, shops closed, even the school was shut down when the heating pipes burst, flooding the classrooms. They rejoiced to be free from school, an extended winter holiday, time to make snowmen, have snow fights, it was great! One of the gang on the road managed to get his hands on the front mud-guard of an old car, and using it as a toboggan, they hurtled down the hill on Botanic Avenue for hours on end. All thoughts of school were suspended for the duration of the snow, and the snow kept coming, wave upon wave till it was impossible to walk the streets in safety. Even the children who revelled in such conditions, began to stay indoors, as the intense cold continued.

Food supplies, megre enough, what with rationing still in place, became even scarcer, as deliveries to the shops ceased. Fuel became a luxury item, to be used sparingly. It was as important as food and just as scarce. Now with the prospect of a few bags of logs to be had, no time was lost in retrieving the box-car from the shed and making it road-worthy.

It was decided to leave the youngest boy Pat with Mrs. Daly, while the three of them set off. Wrapped in the warmest clothes they had, gloves, mufflers, two pairs of socks, he was grateful to be in long trousers. Overnight there had been a very heavy frost, making conditions underfoot treacherous and dangerous. It was their feet that were worse affected by the cold. The rubber boots were good for keeping feet dry but the cold seemed to rise up like an invisible cloak, chilling their very souls.

With a great deal of slipping and sliding the box-car was dragged out on to the snow covered road and pointed in the direction of town. After a few futile attempts at pushing, it was found much easier to pull the box-car in the deep snow. Not a soul was to be seen, just the empty windows staring out as they made their way through the snow, they crossed to the other side of Drumcondra Road. on to the footpath along the tree covered wall of the Bishop's Palace that offered some respite from the bitter cold.

'Does the Bishop have to go for logs mammy?', he innocently asked.

'Somehow or other, I don't think so', replied his mother, John Charles was not her favourite person.

Out from the protection of the trees at Clonliffe Road, it really came down, making bad conditions even worse. Approaching Binn's Bridge, the snow mercifully eased, giving some relief. It stuck to the wheels making it almost impossible to pull, having to stop every few minutes to clear the wheels of the box-car that were caked with snow. At least it was a break from pulling and pushing, and gave them an opportunity to blow on their frozen hands to try and restore the circulation.

As they approached the 'Norrier', others began to appear heading in the same direction. His mother urged them to even greater efforts in fear that the limited supplies of logs would be exhausted before they arrived. Finally the Arch came into view and a queue of people huddled beneath it that afforded some protection from the elements. The pale white faces of the people reflected the colour of the snow. Most were poorly dressed with their shabby clothes and footwear offering little comfort from the rigours of the savage winter.

Slowly each person received their quota which was then loaded on to a bicycle, a hand cart, ancient prams, anything. Some of the less fortunate on their backs, with conditions under foot so treacherous, manys the fall was had before home was reached.

'How many bags do you want, Missus?', asked the thin faced fuel merchant, as he loaded each bag on to the scales, each bag weighing 4 stone.

'Three bags please,' answered his mother.

'Are you sure missus, there is a lot of weight in three bags?', asked the merchant.

'Don't worry mister, we'll manage', was her reply.

With the help of the fuel merchant the bags were loaded on to the box-car and secured with a length of rope. A great effort was required to get the box-car to move but once started the weight of the logs propelled it forward; Being slightly down hill increased the momentum and it nearly ran away with them. Everything was great till they reached Binn's Bridge, the box-car, in spite of their best efforts got bogged down in the snow, and try as they might, nothing would move it. They heaved, pushed, shoved but to no avail.

All the while, the cold increased, it filtered up through their boots, into every bone in their bodies, the woolen gloves, now soaked from trying to free the snow crusted box-car, offered little in the way of comfort.

'Do you want a hand there Missus?,' asked a small, stocky man standing on the footpath watching their attempt to move the box-car. His cap was pulled down around his ears, a heavy overcoat reaching to his heels, his brown hob nail boots barely visible. He reached out with both hands to give the snow bound car a heave.

'All together, now, push', he called.

The box-car jumped forward catching them all by surprise and they sprawled on the snow, sitting there up to their ears in snow, the man started to laugh, they all joined in, it was all so stupid, but it lifted their spirits.

'Missus, this kind of work is not for a woman. It's far too heavy, where is your husband?', inquired the kind man, as they stood brushing the snow from their clothes.

'He's working in England, like a lot of other men', answered his mother. 'We have to do the best we can.' She thanked the kind man for his help, and they set off again on the last leg of their journey. Once over the bridge, it was straight pushing and shoving, each of them taking turns between the shafts. His mother was magnificent, showing great courage and strength, never complaining, leading by example, just doing what had to be done, offering only encouragement.

It was a tired and exhausted family that finally turned the corner into Botanic Avenue, still the endless snow kept coming down. With their freezing hands they unloaded the precious bags from the now creaking box-car, and manhandled the logs into the safety of the house. They were for the present assured of some form of heat, Glimmer man or no Glimmer man, that dreadful winter of 1947.

With some of the gang.

CHAPTER 12

That Last Summer

THEY were free, free at last! The last day at school. It was over, the day they had looked forward to for months, for years. No more exercise, school bags, and best of all, no more Christian Brothers. Just a long, glorious summer to enjoy. They each vowed to throw their school bags and books into the canal on the way home, not that they did, most had younger brothers or sisters who were going to need them. It was a truly wonderful feeling, not for one moment did they give any consideration to what was to be next in their lives. The world was a great place and leaving school was the most important thing in their short lives. The first few weeks were heaven, playing football from morning till night, never tiring, some evenings they would just lie on the grass, savouring the moments, talking football. What else was there in the world?. It was the only sport available to them. Sports such as rugby, basketball, or cricket were unheard of. As for tennis, it was only accessible to members of private clubs, entry to such clubs was the preserve of the middle class. Gaelic games, no self respecting city boy would be caught dead playing Gaelic, everyone knew that it was only for country people.

If the weather was really good, they went swimming in the river Tolka, spending hours sliding down the waterfall and watching the older boys swimming. None of the gang could swim very well, but that did not stop their enjoyment. Occasionally, they would get on their bikes, those who had one and head for Dollymount to try and swim in the sea. The sea water was supposed to be easier for swimming, but that was not their experience.

The cinema was place of reverence, where they entered the magic world of films, and the never to be forgotten 'following-uppers'. Who could ever forget 'The Clutching Hand', or 'Burn-em-up-Barnes'. Real cowboys such as Johnny McBrown, William Boyd as 'Hopalong Cassidy'. The likes of Roy Rogers or Gene Autry were not considered real cowboys, what with their singing and kissing girls, cowboys how are you!

One of his biggest problems was getting into the cinema at the children's matinee. Being tall for his age, he had great difficulty convincing the doorman that he was in fact under age. Mostly it depended on which doorman was on duty. When a certain man was on, he would go along the queue checking the boys, and if in his opinion he thought you were over the age, you got turfed out. Sometimes, by pretending to be small by crouching down, he might fool the doorman and get away with it, more times, he was out on his ear. When that happened, he just went home. He received a shilling from his mother to be divided between his two brothers and himself. At fourpence each, the cost of a childs seat, the next seat price was seven pence – a king's ransom.

Another place of pleasure for him was the Public Library. With plenty of time to spare, he read everything he could get his hands on, Jack London, Oliver Strange and of course Zane Grey, he read everyone of his books that were available from the Library. When they had any money, which was not too often, the gang went to the local 'Milk-bar', for a glass of milk and a cream bun – they thought they were the 'bees-knees'.

That afternoon was a special day, their local team, Drumcondra were playing their arch rivals Shamrock Rovers in nearby Tolka Park, a match not to be missed. Large crowds of men in flat caps and working clothes come directly from work, having satisfied their corporal needs in the many pubs along the way. It was rarely that a woman was seen at a soccer match. Programme sellers, dealers, bicycle attendants vieing with each other for a piece of the action. The bicycle attendants with their make-shift peaked cap, usually a discarded 'busman's' cap, that afforded him a certain air of authority, urging one and all to trust the safety of their bikes to their safe keeping. No money accepted till after the match, when the coloured ticket was presented and the bike retrieved.

The ever present and hardworking dealers, who, having pushed a heavily laden pram of fruit from the city center with innumerable children clinging to the pram, hoping to sell some of the fruit.

'Two apples a penny, Mister, get your fresh apples', was the constant and sometimes plaintiff cry, hoping to dispose of as much as possible, and so avoid having to push the loaded pram back to the city center.

They were a truly remarkable, heroic and resilient breed of women, a law unto themselves. Whatever the event, regardless of the weather conditions, they could be seen peddling their wares. The husband of a dealer was a kept man who enjoyed a privileged life style at his wife's expense, his only apparent contribution to the family was to sire as many children as possible, a task he manfully performed, considering the number of children in each family. Like 'Burlington Bertie', he rose at ten thirty when the streets were well aired, before putting in an appearance, an expensive 'Anthony Eden' hat, a Crombie, overcoat, white silk scarf with matching gloves completed the picture.

He would stroll each morning, like a gentleman of leisure to the nearest 'Bookies'*. The only thing missing was a cane to keep the dogs at bay. His good wife, having left early for the market to purchase the fruit in an effort to provide a subsistence for the family. He could be observed at any sporting fixture, dressed to kill, while his poor wife went about trying to sell as much as possible. Just before the match started, he could be discreetly observed sidling up to his wife to put the hammer on her for the entrance fee, plus the price of a few pints after the match. His appearance and mode of dress reflected her standing in their community, the better dressed he was, the greater her status

The mad rush to the turnstiles when the whistle announced that the match had started, was followed by his rejection at the boys gate for being over age, just like at the cinema.

'Will you go way out of that you are a hairy looking 14', said the voice behind the grill. 'The last time you saw 14 was on the back of a bus'.

'But, Mister, I won't be 14 till next May', he protested vigorously, knowing that he could not afford the adult price. He tried to get a lift over the stile, as was the practice but failed. Turning quickly, he raced up Richmond Road followed by others in the same boat as himself to Drumcondra Road over the bridge and into the grounds of the Bishop's Palace that bounded the river Tolka.

A series of haphazard and dangerous stepping stones laid in the river bed afforded a rather risky means of crossing the river to the football ground on the other side. Taking the precaution of removing his shoes and socks, just in case, before venturing on to the wobbly stones, he took a deep breath, blessed himself, then a quick lunge that carried him without mishap to the other side, his example was followed by the rest of the gang. Sitting on the bank replacing his shoes and socks, he was almost trampled to death by other 'school boys' in a mad rush to get in for nothing.

He glanced up the steep embankment to see if the coast was clear. So far so good, no attendant in sight. The climb up the slippery slope was complicated by the fact that it served as an unofficial convenience. To get wet crossing the river was a natural hazard, to get drenched from above by some character relieving himself after indulging his thirst on the way to the match, was the risk one had to take for not having the entrance fee. It was a relief to reach the summit dry, having run the gauntlet of a man-made waterfall.

Once in the safety of the crowded stand and a vantage point secured, the fact that he had got in for nothing, only increased his enjoyment of the match. Intense rivalry existed between the supporters of each team, with many a noisy and heated exchange of views, but most of the abuse was directed at the unfortunate referee. Whatever dispute there was between the different supporters. It was generally agreed that the referee's pedigree, like some of his decisions were to say the least, questionable. A good sense of humour also prevailed, one incident illustrates this side of the game. A visiting player at one stage of the game, head back, was going flat out chasing a ball he had no chance of catching, when a wag in the crowd loudly cried out. 'Open the gates', reducing the players, referee and the crowd to a state of hysterical laughter.

In the modern game, one seldom sees a player smile, it is all taken far too seriously. The local hero was the enigmatic Benny Henderson, in his eyes the greatest player in the land, a tall, elegant, slightly stooped winger, the sweetest striker of a ball you ever did see. He could transform a game with just one strike of the ball. That day he lived up to his reputation by scoring the winning goal with a wicked drive that almost decapitated the unfortunate goalkeeper, sending him home ecstatic, having beaten their great rivals, and not costing him a penny.

Those few anxious days leading to the great event had finally come to pass, was this to be their year. Would their dreams at last be realised? There had been many close calls along the way, from the start of the campaign to the 1946 Cup final (attendance 34,248). Now the fateful day had arrived and their team, Drumcondra was to meet their arch rivals, Shamrock Rovers. They were at full strength, there could be no excuse this time. Had they not decisively beaten Rovers only a few weeks before? The long wait between Mass and dinner, a dinner that was eaten, more out of respect for his mother than anything else. He had arranged to join up with his pals outside Coffey's shop and they were soon on their way to Dalymount Park, along with thousands of others, all heading in the same direction and with only one thing in mind, the match. The closer they got to the ground, the greater the numbers, with all the usual characters about the place, bicycle attendants, dealers, and a variety of street sellers, peddling their wares, coloured scarves and hats, all trying to make a few shillings. Long queues had formed at each of the turnstiles, even the schoolboys gate had a huge number of 'schoolboys' some of whom, were, to say the least, badly in need of a shave.

Some wore short pants in an attempt to deceive the turnstile men into thinking they were under fourteen, but there hairy legs, were a dead give away. In spite of the fact that he was still under fourteen but tall for his age, he approached the turnstile with trepidation, between two other 'schoolboys', who were at least a couple of years older than himself, fearful of being turned away. If that happened, he was sunk, the extra cost of an adult ticket was for him, out of sight. He crouched as low as he could, making himself as small as possible passing through the hatch, right behind the 'schoolboy' in front of him, who was admitted without question, and so was he.

Relieved, he joined the rest of the gang at the foot of the concrete steps that led to the open terraces above. There was no separate enclosure for children, they were obliged to find there own space.

Somehow they managed to find a safe place in front of a steel safety barrier, having been warned by their parents of the dangers in such a crowded place. With more than a hour before kick-off, the crowd was still pouring in and being marshalled to the back of the terraces by the few hapless attendants. On to the pitch came the St. James Gate Brass Band to entertain the crowd, they were a regular feature at all the big matches. Their conductor, a flamboyant character, stepped it out in front of the band with a high stepping gait, his long staff setting the tempo. Beginning in front of the reserved stand, they set off in tight formation, playing the usual marching music. On reaching the end of the pitch, the conductor, with a wave and a flourish of his staff, marched on the spot to form an orderly turn.

This was greeted by a great cheer from the spectators and the routine was repeated at each corner of the ground, almost as if there was a competition to see which section of the crowd was the loudest. As the hour approached, the band came to a halt in front of the stand, in preparation for the arrival of the teams. Both teams marched out of the tunnel in single file and lined up in the center of the pitch, standing to attention for the National Anthem. The band, having completed their programme of music, were hustled off the pitch and down the dark tunnel. The referee's whistle signalled the start of the game, the real business of the day had commenced. The match started at a frantic pace and within a minute, Rovers were in front with a goal scored by their captain, Paddy Coad. His heart sank, to be behind after only one minute, this was not how they it was supposed to be. The football was mostly kick and rush, end too end, with little effort to play good football, not that the spectators noticed or cared, they could see nothing wrong with their teams performance. It took a while before Drums regained their composure and began to come back in to the game.

They equalised after about ten minutes with a goal by Tommy Mc Cormack, that settled the nerves. Almost immediately, from the back of the terraces, came a great surge forward by a section of spectators, that drove everyone in its path, down the concrete steps, like a human avalanche, crushing the spectators at the front against the perimeter wall. Fortunately no one was hurt, but it was to become an unwelcome feature of the game in different parts of the ground. Whenever something occurred close to the touch line, the people at the back of the terraces would push forward to see what was happening, with the inevitable result. Himself and his pals, situated as they were in front of the barrier, escaped the dangerous heave but not by much, they were close enough to witness what could have been a serious situation. From then to half-time, many chances were wasted by both sides, especially Rovers, who fritted away chance after chance, something they would regret. Despite being packed in like sardines, someone always had to relieve themselves, having hung on as long as they could, in fear of missing something taking place on the pitch, they had to move. This entailed climbing down a steep bank to reach the toilet and climbing back up again, with not a hope of finding your place in the crowd. Some spectators preferred to forgo the trip and instead, relieved themselves where they stood, a practice known locally as 'warm-leg', a despicable thing to do, that sometimes resulted in a dispute with the other more responsible spectators.

The rivalry between opposing supporters was friendly, with each trying to out do the other in their own way, but still retaining their passionate belief in their own team. By half-time, Drums were lucky to be on equal terms, and as the whistle sounded for the break, the players trooped off the field, a welcome break for them and with their passing, the band returned for a short ten minute interval recital. Polite applause greeted their rendering of an obscure overture, it was only when the strains of Strauss's 'Blue Danube' were heard, that the crowd sat up and began to take notice. But not in the way one would have expected them to. When the opening notes were sounded, the crowd responded by adding their own words, certainly not as the composer had intended,

'It's all on your leg—gick—gick—la—la'.

'It's six inches thick—gick—gick—la—la'.

A not very polite way to treat a serious piece of music, but it expressed the festive mood of the day. The conductor, knowing he was on to a good thing, repeated the chorus, much to the enjoyment of the crowd, who raised their voices to a higher level. Reluctantly the band completed their programme and retired to the dressing room, to thunderous applause, delighted, no doubt, that for once, their efforts had been appreciated, even if it was in a rather oblique fashion. The match resumed, and the second half went the same way, with Rovers taking the match to Drums, but they had a resolute defence and frustrated Rovers every move. The game dragged on with Drums on the receiving end most of the time. Just when it appeared that a draw was inevitable, one moment of magic by his favourite player, won the match. Benny Henderson the tall winger, collected the ball in the center of the field and as the Rovers defence backed off, he let fly with a shot that swerved and turned, leaving Jimmy Collins, in the Rovers goal stranded. A 'banana' shot, long before the Brazilians were ever heard of. The goal was greeted with a huge sigh of relief by the Drums supporters, who at that stage in the game were beginning to lose heart. From then on, it was just a matter of hanging on, playing out time. For himself and his pals, it was to be the longest half- hour of their lives. Every kick was greeted with a cheer. Agonisingly they counted the minutes on the St. Peters' Church clock tower, as it edged its way, ever so slowly to the magical, ten past five and victory. Finally the whistle sounded to take then out of their misery. They cheered with the presentation of the F.A.I. Cup and for each member of the team when they received their winners medal.

With the packed crowd tumbling down the steps, always there was some guy trying to get back into the ground, pushing his way, up the steps, against the tide of bodies leaving the stadium. He could never understand why?. The match was over, the Cup was won, there was nothing in the ground but waste paper and cigarette butts. The same thing occurred at every match he ever went to, always there was some guy who tried to get back into the deserted ground, he often wondered why. Their feet hardly touched the ground as they headed for home, their first Cup final had been a winning one. The Gods had indeed smiled on them.

Occasionally when swimming he overheard the older boys talking, using expressions like a 'Brasser'* or 'A Brass nail'. 'She was on the town', or 'On the game.' When he queried what they meant, he was impolitely told to 'get lost', to come back when he was older. Now and then, someone would make reference to girls, but for most of the gang, it was a no go subject, they were never mentioned. Anyone who played with girls was a cissy, everyone knew that. Unconsciously they avoided the subject, afraid to face the inevitable. Like most Irishmen, they never felt comfortable in the company of women, they were safe in their own gang, hoping it would last forever, nothing ever does.

Everything in their upbringing and education was designed to separate boys and girls, the influence of a celibate Catholic church was all pervading. Ironically they were totally unaware of the facts of life, even though most of them had just finished their education. Some of them still believed that babies were found under a head of cabbage, that was the extent of their ignorance. Girls had a better understanding of the changes, both physical and psychological, but for boys, it was not so clear cut.

The summer rolled on, the good times continued, it turned out to be a fine summer for a change, for most of them, the last fine summer they were to experience for a long time. In many ways the turning point in their lives, school was finished for all of them, what next? This idyll was shattered one day as they rested in the park, talking football as usual, when a young girl just walked over and sat down right in the middle of the circle and began talking. There was much confusion in the ranks. It turned out she was an English girl over on holidays, staying with her aunt for the summer. Never before had any of the local girls come within a mile of them, they certainly got no encouragement from the boys, a bunch of slobs, caught between boys and adolescence, unaware of the changes taking place.

Her funny accent made it difficult to understand what she was saying, but the effect on the gang was immediate, to say the least. Some reacted by saying nothing, hoping she would just go back to England, leave them as they were to enjoy their last summer holiday together. Others responded differently, enjoying her company, it was hard to tell if it was bravado or something deeper. Each of them was trying to adjust to the changes, taking place in their lives, unaware of what was happening – they were growing up but did not know it!

After the first encounter with the English girl, the next few weeks saw subtle changes take place, the appearance of some of the gang improved, hair that had for years been left to its own devices was suddenly combed, even slicked down, more noticeable were the shoes. They were getting polished every day and not just for Mass on Sunday. For a while, most of them went along with the situation, but when it became an everyday occurrence, one of them was heard to remark that at this rate none of them would have a stitch of clothes in their wardrobe, that's if any of them even had a wardrobe. By this time, the local girls began putting in an appearance each time the English girl came on the scene, they obviously enjoyed the chance to mix with the boys. There was some friction between brothers and sisters, each threatening to tell their respective parents, that so-and-so was playing with girls, something frowned upon by most parents.

The real problem was that they had nothing in common on which to agree or even discuss, the boys were all about football, the girls had no interest in sport whatsoever, they played skipping or beds, not the kind of games any self respecting boy would be caught dead playing. A lot of good natured slagging took place, some of the girls had their hair pulled, especially those unlucky enough to have 'pig-tales', they would pretend to be hurt and would walk away, saying, 'I'm going home', but would only go a short distance, before rejoining the group.

A subject they all had in common was school but nobody dared mention it, certainly not the boys. Most of whom attended the Christian Brother's, something they preferred to forget, having suffered at the hands of the same Brother's, and had the marks to prove it. The cinema the only subject they all could relate to, it became the talking point, that they could not agree on any of the films, was predictable but at least it was a start. As the summer wore on, the football matches became less frequent, didn't seem so important after all. They sensed, unconsciously, that they were entering a new phase in their, so far, uncomplicated lives. In a few short weeks, the whole pattern of their lives seemed to change, it would never be the same again.

He took the easy way out, by taking refuge in the Public Library.

One of the strangest things that happened to him that summer, he developed a passion for, of all things, cricket! How this manifest itself, is still a mystery, it was so far removed from anything he had ever done before, never ever having seen a cricket match, as for playing it, not a chance, it was the preserve of the middle class. With the football season over for the summer and with nothing better to do, he tuned into the B.B.C. Light programme and as luck would have it, the first test match between England and the Australians had just commenced. This turned out to be the first Australian team to tour since the end of the war. Perhaps it was the deep, melodious, knowledgeable voice of the commentator, John Arlott, but whatever it was, he was hooked. He learned that strange vocabulary, a vocabulary that only the English could invent, with names such as, 'silly mid off', 'short leg', 'bowling a maiden over', 'body line' a 'googly', and many other weird and wonderful expressions. The names of the players are still indelibly impressed on his mind to this day; Bradman, Lindwall, Miller, Tallon to name but a few Australians. On the English side, there was Hutton, Compton, Evans, Bedser among many others, some of the finest players ever to grace the game. Don Bradman was the most famous Aussie. The greatest batsman of his time, the unforgettable and moving experience of his last test match when he was bowled out for a 'duck' by Holles, will remain in his heart forever. John Arlott's vivid and moving description of that fateful event, when he spoke in hushed, solemn terms, like a religious ceremony, was so eloquent at the passing of a sporting legend.

When that 'Last Summer' finally came to an end, each went their separate ways, some went to work, others to Tech. One even went to secondary school, a rare occurrence in those days, No more long summer days with nothing to do, except to enjoy every moment, they realised it was over for them. It was to be two weeks holidays a year, it they were lucky to find a job. Most considered themselves lucky, at least they had an opportunity to enjoy a blissful childhood in peace and safety, unlike thousands of displaced children in war-torn Europe.

Drama group

CHAPTER 13

Going to Tech

THE summer drew to it's inevitable conclusion, minds focused on the alarming prospect of another winter. Few relished the thought, the hardship endured that dreadful winter of 1947, had left its mark, particularly on children and the elderly. Rationing was still a way of life, white bread, oranges, bananas, even coal a distant memory. The days slipped quietly, gently by, autumn began to show on the brown leafed trees, reminding all that it was time to take stock.

His acceptance by the Tech* in Denmark Street arrived without warning. Having survived Primary school the Tech had to be an improvement, the prospect of school without Christian Brothers raised his expectations, still it took some time to adjust to the more enlightened atmosphere of the Tech.

Tech was magic. For a start, he was treated as a person, not as just a name on a page, some of the teachers even went so far as to address the pupils by their first name. The effect on the boys was immediate, they opened up and began to shed a lot of imposed insecurities. It manifest itself in their readiness to learn, with the threat of corporal punishment removed, they began to respond to the teachers, even the dreaded Irish was accepted gracefully. None more so than himself, the freedom to express oneself without fear of the consequences, brought him out of his timid self, so much so, that he was in due course elected class captain.

The range and variety of subjects exceeded his wildest expectations of what school should be; as well as maths, Irish, woodwork, metalwork, drawing, both freehand and mechanical, to say nothing of P.E. (physical exercise),. And horror of horrors, for English there was a Lady teacher, the redoubtable Miss Kelly. The P.E. teacher, Reggie Myles, really laid into the boys for the first few weeks, he had them running, jumping, doing press-ups and many other hard exercises. In no time it was on to the parallel bars and the vaulting horse, they were young men in the making, and it came easy to them. Except one poor, harmless young fella, nick-named 'Bubbles' who had no co-ordination whatsoever, he just could not do even basic exercises no matter how hard he tried. His inability to even walk properly used to drive Reggie wild. When walking, his right arm and leg went forward together, likewise with his left hand and foot, like a toy soldier.

None of them had ever seen the inside of a Gym. and it gave them a certain status with their pals to be able to say that they had worked out in a real Gym. One of the healthiest looking boys in the class, apple red cheeks, fine complexion and all, presented Reggie with a doctor's medical certificate advising against any form of psyical exercise. Reggie's reaction was both immediate and predictable, given the kind of man he was, with little sympathy for what he perceived as a slacker.

'You mean to stand there, with your bare face hanging down like that and suggest that you are unable to do any P.E?', inquired Reggie, holding the medical cert. aloft for all the class to see.

'Yes, Sir,' answered the boy nervously, 'My mammy says it is too hard for me'.

'Pray tell me why that is so?', said Reggie, knowing full well that there was nothing he could do about the medical cert.

'I don't know, Sir', replied the boy in an uncertain voice. He was dodging the column and they all knew it.

'You are indeed excused' said Reggie sarcastically, 'but if you think for one minute that you are going to. have a handy few hours every week, you have another think coming'.

He was frog marched to a desk in the corner and given a composition to write on 'Why I could not do P.E.'

To have a lady teacher after years of being ruled by the Brothers took some getting used to, some of them wondered at the need for an English teacher. 'Don't we all know how to speak English!', one boy was heard to remark, a view shared by a number of the class. Miss Kelly, to her eternal credit, managed to focus their attention by not using the usual, boring school textbooks. Instead they read Treasure Island, and Coral Island, books that young boys could relate to. Each day a chapter was read and discussed in detail, in marked contrast to any previous learning experience. So much so, that every boy in the class had the book read and understood within a few weeks, something unheard of in primary school.

They were encouraged to discuss the events in the books, it was quite amazing to listen to the suggestions put forward and the enthusiasm generated in such a short space of time. It opened up a lot of the boys, brought them out of themselves after the suffocating years in primary school.

He responded to this new openness by getting involved in everything, sport, debates, even a play. Miss Kelly managed to persuade a very reluctant class to perform a play in Irish entitled, 'An Rí a Bhi Breoite', (The King who was sick), complete with wigs, and fancy costumes. After their collective experience at the hands of the Brothers, to put it mildly, Irish was not a favourite subject. He was chosen to play the part of the sick King, mostly because he was tall, and of equal importance, the costume fitted him perfectly! Other members of the cast were not so lucky. They even took part in the Féis Ceoil,* and received a prize for their efforts.

She even had the nerve to try and teach them Shakespeare! Can you just imagine a crowd of 'Gurriers'* trying to do King John, with such memorable lines as, 'Wilt thou with hot irons burn out both myne eyes', 'Young boy I must', 'And wilt thou? 'And I will'. Can you think of anything more ridiculous in all your life? But strange as it may seem, it worked, and they actually enjoyed it.

Miss Kelly, God bless her innocence as part of her desire to improve our knowledge of English, insisted that the class assemble outside the Tech on a Wednesday afternoon, in spite of the fact that it was a half-day, to go and see a film version of Shakespeare's 'Hamlet' showing in the Carlton cinema in O'Connell Street starring Laurence Olivier. For weeks Miss Kelly had been singing the praises of Shakespeare's language and its relevance to life. It was with no great expectations they gathered outside the Tech with most of them bemoaning the fact that it was a half day off, and like sheep going through a gap, they marched behind Miss Kelly to the cinema. Each in their turn purchased a ticket and headed down the long passageway to the cheapest seats in the half- empty cinema. For the next few hours they sat through one of the most boring films ever seen. Most of the difficulty stemmed from their inability to understand the 'old' English of Shakespeare. To them the acting was very oriented and as for the long soliloquies, made no sense at all and were completely over their heads. They would have preferred a war or a cowboy picture, at least they could have followed the plot and with no fancy language to cope with. To most of the class, even the 'Three Stooges' would have been better, they would have got a few laughs for their money. Following their visit to the cinema, Miss Kelly was in raptures for weeks, so much so, that she overlooked giving homework, so all was not lost. They had gained something from the experience, even if not culturally.

As much as he enjoyed most classes, he came into his own in the woodwork class, taking it like a 'fly to a cow pat' It seemed to come easy, so natural working with timber, it was obvious to the teacher that he was destined to be associated in some capacity with the trade. In every practical exercise they were obliged to undertake, he completed the task quickly and well, even offering assistance to other less capable boys, when the teacher was not looking, of course.

Half-way through the second year, he was approached by the woodwork teacher, Mr Cooney who asked him if he was interested in an apprenticeship to a Joiner.

'I have a friend of mine who has a joinery shop and is looking for an apprentice, are you interested?'

'Yes Sir,' he answered, excited at the prospect of a job, 'but I will have to ask my parents first'.

'You do that', replied Mr. Cooney. 'Let me know as soon as you can'.

He could not wait for lunch hour to come, racing home to tell his mother the news, his feet hardly touched the ground, arriving home breathless, much to his mother's surprise.

'What's wrong?', she asked, suspecting trouble, as only a mother can. 'What are you doing home this hour of the day?'

'Nothing's wrong, Mammy', he replied, still breathless from running. 'The teacher asked me if I wanted to serve my time as a Joiner'.

'You mean as an apprentice', she answered with surprise in her voice.

'Please Mammy, can I?', he pleaded.

'Certainly you can', confirmed his mother, relieved to get some good news for a change. 'When does he want a reply'?.

'Right away, Mammy', he said anxiously. 'Today if possible'.

'But what about your father? He should be consulted about things like that', his mother replied.' It will take a week for a letter to go to England and back'.

'But Mammy, the job might not be there next week', he cried, fearful of a lost opportunity, not realising the pressure he was placing on his mother.

She sank down into a chair and sighed deeply. 'What am I going to do? If only your father was here.'

She had laboured long and hard to rear three boys, more or less on her own, what with wartime restrictions, rationing, seeing her husband once or twice a year, those hours spent knitting woolen jumpers, as she sought to supplement the family income. He can still hear the gentle clicking of knitting needles, that went on long into the night. In spite of having coped with all these problems, now she was being asked to decide in a few minutes her eldest son's future, it was proving to be just too much for her. Whatever decision that was arrived at now, she would have to live with it for the rest of her days.

'Are you sure this is what you want to do?' she asked, fearful of the reply.

'Yes, I always wanted to be a tradesman', he answered firmly.

The following day he arranged with Mr. Cooney to go and see about the job. It was with heightened expectations, he approached the workshop in Nottingham Street on the North Strand, only to find the door half-open, so he entered quietly, not knowing what to expect. The low-roofed building seemed crowded with woodworking machines, the likes of which he had never seen before, machines he was to become all so familiar with. A thick layer of white dust covered everything, that gave the place a Christmas like appearance including the owner, a Mr. Russell. to whom he was introduced by Mr. Cooney. He was a heavy set man with the upper rim of his soft hat filled with shavings and saw dust, a pair of bushy, white covered eyebrows overhanging thick bottle-end glasses and the inevitable stub of a cigarette stuck between his lips completed the picture. After a few basic questions, a starting wage of one pound was agreed, with a firm handshake. He was to start his apprenticeship that following Monday.

Typical hand-cut roof with dormer.

CHAPTER 14

The Joiners Apprentice

HIS mother had managed to get the loan of a bike from his uncle, till he could afford one himself, so off he went that first morning, a new tool box hastily put together tied to the carrier with a few basic tools rattling inside. Down Richmond Road to Ballybough and on to the workshop in Nottingham Steet on the most important day in his life. Mr. Russell greeted him with a gruffness he was too become only to familiar with. He was a little disappointed to learn that apart from Mr. Russell, he was the only one working in the shop, he had expected to be working with other Joiners, though it was not to be.

He was introduced to a noisy, dust creating sanding machine with a revolving belt for finishing joinery. The items to be sanded were first placed on a flat tray, that was then pushed in and out with one hand, the other hand pressed down a pad on to the revolving sand belt. Needless to say, it took some time to get accustomed to the workings of the machine. In the course of sanding a four-panel door, he somehow managed to catch the belt in the door, and with a mighty bang, the long belt snapped and went crashing all over the place.

He jumped back with fright, before switching off the machine. Mr.Russell quickly came to his assistance, the belt was repaired, nothing was said, just an awkward silence, something he was to become accustomed to over the years. He was simply afraid to speak, he had inside an hour, almost wrecked a machine; was he to be dismissed with not even a day's work behind him, with no comment from Mr.Russell, what was he really thinking? He was just left to ponder his fate. The machine was restarted and with no further accidents, he settled down and soon got the hang of the machine.

By lunch hour, like everything else in the place, he was covered by a thin layer of white dust. He was feeling tired, his feet ached from standing in the same spot for hours on end, the break was most welcome. His sparkling new 'Billy' can boiled quickly on the gas ring and he settled down to enjoy the sandwiches. Mr. Russell left to have lunch with his sister, who lived down the street.

It was not exactly as he had envisaged, he had expected to be working and dining with others, talking football and other topics of the day, instead he found himself alone. Still it was a start. At 1.30. precisely he resumed work, pausing only to remove some doors and sashes that were finished. Occasionally Mr. Russell inquired as to how he was getting along, he solderied on for the rest of the afternoon. Approaching five o'clock, finishing time, he eyed the ancient dust covered wall clock. Waiting for it to pass the magic hour, it seemed to take forever, the minutes were endless. Finally the minute hand crossed over and to his amazement, it dropped to almost ten past five. This being his first day, he hesitated before switching off the machine, fearing that he be taken for a slacker.

Cycling home that evening, a little tired but elated, he received a few odd glances from people in the street, it was only when he arrived home did he realise that he had the loveliest pair of white eyebrows imaginable. Came Friday and his first pay day, it was with great pride that he handed his pay packet to his mother unopened, at last he was in a position to contribute to the family. Never again would he have to rely on his parents for everything. His mother graciously accepted the pay packet, and returned 5 shillings to him for his pocket money. It was an enormous amount, more than he had ever received before. He finally managed to save enough money to get his very own bike, a dark green Raleigh Retriever, complete with 3 speed-gears and a carrier, which served him well over the years.

At the end of his first year he was accepted into the Carpenter's Union, the A.S.W.* who advised him of the current rates of pay for a second year apprentice. The very thought of approaching Mr. Russell to seek a pay rise, scared him for weeks. He would prepare the speech, word for word and practice against the background of a noisy machine, but when the time came to breech the subject with Mr.Russell his courage deserted him. This situation continued for weeks, he just did not have the nerve to ask. Each week his mother asked the same question.' Did you ask Mr. Russell about the pay rise'?. and each week he would fob her off with 'I didn't get time', or ' I forgot to ask'. Finally she laid it on the line for him,' Either you ask or I will go myself'. Caught between two forces and with the prospect of his mother's intervention, he was shamed into making a move.

One evening as he was about to leave, in sheer desperation, he knocked on the office door and gently opened it. Before Mr. Russell could open his mouth, he blurted out his over prepared speech.

'Sir, my mother says now that I am my 2nd year, I am entitled to a 5 shilling increase'.

Mr. Russell just stared at him through his dust covered glasses. After what seemed an eternity, with one last drag from a cigarette, he slowly removed the stub from his mouth and crushed it into a well filled ash tray beside him.

'Is that it?, came the short reply.

'Yes, Sir', he gasped, thankful that he was wearing long trousers, his knees were knocking together like marbles on a piece of glass.

'I'll see what I can do', was the cryptic answer he got, giving nothing away.

With great relief he turned away and out the door and as quick as his wobbly legs would carry him, cycling home, his knees still shaking from the ordeal. He consoled himself that the problem had been faced up to, at least for this year. It was to become an annual event, the source of much soul searching for him, the only consolation was, that the following week he received the extra money.

The volume of work increased considerably, necessitating an extra pair of hands. There arrived one morning without warning, Tom, an older brother of Mr. Russell. To say they were different is an understatement of the highest order, if ever there were two opposites, these pair certainly were. Mr. Russell, quiet, passive, non-drinking, speaking only when necessary, he went about his work with almost mechanical precision, everything down to the last detail. Tom on the other hand, was loud, noisy, and careless about his work, his overzealous use of the hammer was not appreciated by his brother. Of medium build, with a yellow stained moustache and a mischievous glint in his grey eyes, he seemed to take great pleasure in getting up his brother's nose. His language was horrendous, if anything went against him, he would light up the place with a string of adjectives not found in an Oxford dictionary. Mr. Russell would cringe with embarrassment and discomfort at his brother's outbursts. Still, it was like a breath of fresh air for him, having someone to talk to, even if he was old enough to be his grandfather.

Lunch hour came that first day, and Tom was out the door like a flash to the nearest pub, arriving back an hour later, suitably refreshed. At the end of one bench, out of sight, he kept a ready supply of 'Baby-Power's'* that were quickly and expertly dispatched. 'Dead men tell no tales' was his only comment! The overpowering smell of whiskey permeated the workshop, even the potent smell of boiling glue failed to overcome it. Tom would speak of the so called 'good old days' working on various building sites, of rogue builders. He reserved his choicest language for so-called foremen, 'bastards one and all', he would mutter out loud.

One quiet afternoon, Tom asked, 'Did you ever hear of Sean Russell?'

'No', he replied

'Well, he was the head of the I.R.A. before the war', answered Tom, nodding his bushy head.' Died on board a German submarine on his way home'.

'What happened to him, was he killed by the Germans'?. he inquired with surprise in his voice.

'Died of natural causes is what we were told',. replied Tom. 'He was my younger brother, he used to work here. See all those tools over there, his name is inscribed on them, in Irish of course'.

'Strange Mr. Russell never mentioned anything about him to me', he responded, puzzled at the lack of interest shown by Mr. Russell.

'That does not surprise me', replied Tom, 'sometimes I think he has lost the power of speech. Too long in the one place, not good for you'.

Around that time, he was invited to play for a local football team, 'Crusaders'. in the Schoolboys League, most of whose matches were played in the Phoenix Park on Sunday morning. It turned out to be one of the most important events in his life so far. Those football years were the greatest single thing to come his way, even if some of the playing conditions were, to say the least, far from perfect, the sheer enjoyment was unforgettable.

Every Sunday Morning, after Mass, it was off to the Park with his boots to play a match, and with a little luck, they might even get to use one of the few dressing-rooms to change their clothes. More then likely, they would have to undress on the grass and hope it would not rain. If it rained, your clothes got wet, unless someone had the presence of mind to bring a water- proof cape, then all the clothes were stuffed underneath and hope for the best. The sixteen acres can be a very unsociable place on a wet and windy morning. After the match, naturally there was no means of washing oneself, and like the others, he would have to pick the mud from his legs on the way home in the bus.

Having manufactured some joinery for one of their regular builder's, they requested his services from Mr. Russell for him to go on site and second fix the work that had just been completed. At first he was reluctant to go but as Mr. Russell rightly pointed out, experience in all aspects of the trade was essential. One of the many jobs he was farmed out to was erect a series of shelves in a city center clothing factory in Temple Bar. Working on his own, he was surrounded by dozens of young girls his own age, who worked the sewing machines, which was the worst possible location for one of his disposition. He received such a slagging from the girls, who teased him unmercifully, the lengths they went to embarrass were extraordinary, like hiding his tools, or worse, putting ladies unmentionables on his pocket, and the things they said, would have made a sailor blush.

Having been raised in such a close-knit family, with two brothers, there was no contact with girls his own age. He was like someone coming out of a closed religious order, and this being one of his first experiences with girls and the hard time he got he came to hate the very thought of going to work in the factory knowing he would be subjected to an ordeal every day. He just braved it out, since all he wanted was to get the job finished so that he could get back to the safety of the workshop and peace.

One of the oddest jobs that came their way, was the making of 4 very large frame and sheeted doors for the Giraffe House in Dublin Zoo. They were enormous in size, the largest doors they had ever they been asked to make, considering the size of the animals to be housed. Two pair of doors, each door was over 9'-0" high by 6'-0" wide with the sizes and weight of the timber required many times greater than an average door. The very act of putting them together, was real problem. It required the best efforts of four men just to load the doors on to the truck, mercifully they were not called upon to hang the doors in the zoo.

Following his harrowing experience in the clothing factory, he found himself more times than not out on building sites, at first reluctantly, not wishing for a repeat performance, every job brought a new experience, most of all the variety of people was for him a shock, a revelation. The carefree, indulgent attitude of the men, their approach to work, was to say the least, different. They seemed to spend as much time and energy watching out for the foreman as working.

It came as a shock to go on a building site for the first time, nothing or no one had prepared him for what he was about to experience. There was sort of chaos about the whole site, everything appeared to be in a mess, with no apparent plan of action. After parking his bike beside the Foreman's hut, he nearly got trampled in the rush by men in as they rushed to clock in, before the whistle blew.

He introduced himself to the foreman, a loud, boisterous man in his mid fifties, much given to swearing, who called one of the men over.' Dan, here's the young improver I promised you', he said loudly, 'show him the ropes'.

'Sure', replied Dan, who turned and gestured for him to follow.' Bring your tool box and for God's sake, lock your bike, nothing is safe here unless it is nailed to the ground'.

He was a medium built man in his forties, who walked with a firm, deliberate pace, not rushing, not slow, but with a air of independence about him. He was to encounter, over the years, many tradesmen with that similar independent streak, synonymous with the building trade. The casual nature of the work, going from job to job, from employer to employer, often treated badly made them hard and wary. At the whim of the foreman, you could be sacked, regardless of one's ability or skill and your commitment to the job, it was easy to realise how you could become cynical about the trade. They made their way down a half constructed road, with houses at various stages of construction on each side. Eventually they arrived at a semi-detached house that was roofed, with the windows in place but with no glass. Stepping over the debris that littered the place, they entered to find the ground floor joists in place waiting for the flooring.

'For the next few weeks it's flooring', said Dan with a resigned sigh of one who had seen it all before. He drew his hammer, saw and square from his battered old tool box.

Not wishing to appear too dumb, he did likewise and waited for Dan to start. Beginning on the ground floor, they lined up the first board and took it from there.

'Take it from one who knows, it is better to work at a steady pace', stated Dan as they began laying out the tongue and groove boards.' That way, you get more done and you don't have to kill yourself. Some of the young fellas go tear-arcing and by lunch hour they are knackered'. Proceeding at a steady pace, the boards were soon in place, cramped and nailed. As they were about to move to another room on the ground floor, there came a cry from outside, 'He's coming'.

'Who's coming?', he inquired of Dan, curious to find out what was going on.

'It's the foreman', answered Dan with no great enthusiasm.

At that very moment the head of the Foreman appeared through the door.

'How's the improver doing?' he asked Dan.

'We are both doing fine,' replied Dan firmly.

'See you both later,' said the Foreman who turned away and headed down the site in a great hurry'.

'What was that all about?', he asked Dan, still at a loss as to what was going on.

'Well, you see, it's like this,' answered Dan 'most of the fellas fancy a cup of tea around ten o'clock, but tea breaks are not allowed, so they try and sneak a cup on the quiet, especially in winter.'

'What harm is a cup of tea?', he said in disbelief. 'Surely they would perform better after a cup of tea'.

'Try telling that to the Foreman,' retorted Dan bitterly. 'That's why he does the rounds every morning, just in case'.

'What happens if he catches anyone, are they sacked?', he inquired in his ignorance.

'He kicks over the "Billy" can, that's what he does', replied Dan.

'Your joking,' he answered incredulously.

'I'm not, but he would have to be up early in the morning to catch some of the guys on this site,' came the reply from Dan.

'It sounds very petty and childish to me,' he answered shaking his head in disbelief.

'You should see some of the things they get up too, just for a cup of tea,' Dan replied with a smile. 'They start a bogus fire in one of the houses at one end of the site, and when your man comes running to investigate, the real 'Billy' cans are boiling.

'It's hardly worth the trouble,' he stated.

'It's not really the tea, its the principle,' answered Dan. 'The first thing you learn on a building site is, to know exactly where the foreman is at all times. It could cost you your job, not knowing'.

They continued with the flooring, making good progress up to mid-day. A man who introduced himself as the 'Shop Steward', interrupted them, and inquired if he had a Union card, and if so, to produce it for inspection. Lucky for him, he had been advised by his father not to forget his Union card, so he handed it over to the 'Shop Steward', who duly noted his name and number and returned it with thanks.

'You do understand, we have to be ever vigilant,' and away he went down the site. Not to have produced a Union card, a few days grace was given, failing that, you were suspended until you could produce a current card. Lunch-hour, (actually a half hour), was soon upon them and they made their way to the site Canteen. It turned out to be a galvanised shed that also housed bags of cement, into which a large crowd of men tried to squeeze into. The numerous Billy cans were boiled on an open brazier outside and they had to make the best of it, grateful it was not raining. As for sanitary services, the less said the better. An eight foot galvanised hoarding that housed a plank sitting on a few concrete blocks served as a toilet. It seemed rather ironic, that the very tradesmen who installed the sanitary and sewage services to new houses, were themselves denied access to a proper toilet. As a direct result of this, it was quite common to find in newly completed houses that the toilet was pressed into use, even if there was no water to flush them out, with all that implies.

As tough as the job was, it was nothing compared with the general labourers. One could not but admire their resilience, as they spent hours digging out foundations for a new house, by hand, using a pick and shovel. Starting first thing in the morning, they laboured all day in every kind of weather, digging, hacking and shovelling till the required depth had been achieved.

Their secret was in the rhythm they employed working, like mechanical men, at the same pace all day. Others were stuck behind the concrete mixer, turning out concrete for foundations and sand and cement for plasterers, for hours on end. These men also made the concrete blocks on site, using the mixer and a hand machine to make blocks. A gauge of gravel, cement and water, to a prescribed amount, then turned into a hand-pressed mould to form the blocks. The concrete was then compacted in the machine and placed on pallet and left to cure in the open. Always doubts were expressed at the quality and strength of the hand made blocks. Sure it was not beyond some builders to scrimp on the cement, due to its cost.

By late afternoon, his knees and his back began to feel the effects of hours laying floors, he was relieved to hear the whistle blow for five o'clock, it had been a long hard first day, crawling around on his knees. For the remainder of that week and part of the next week, he toiled on floors. That following Sunday, his knees were so tender, that he had to sit out the Mass.

Over the next few months, he worked at a variety of jobs; erecting partitions, fixing skirting, hanging doors, fitting architrave's, door locks, the list was endless. When it came to roofs, he found himself as part of a crew, fixing and securing pre-cut roofs. The roof parts were cut by hand, on the ground, by part of the crew, and fixed in place by the roofing crew. The experience gained was hard psyicially and very demanding but at the same time valuable lessons were learned. There was very little reference made to what he had been taught in Bolton Street. As for the 'steel square', when he mentioned it, it got a laugh. No one had even heard of it, never mind what use could be made of it.

Most of the working conditions on building sites were basic, some were very bad, especially after heavy rain, with mud everywhere. As much as he enjoyed the freedom of working on building sites, he was quite happy to return to the workshop, especially with winter on the way.

During the second year of his apprenticeship, the volume of work increased to such an extent that an extra pair of hands was required to deal with the workload. There was no way that Mr. Russell was going to employ his brother Tom. They were incompatible. There arrived one morning, a young apprentice named Gerry, who had some previous experience at the trade. His arrival changed the whole atmosphere of the place, at last he had someone of his own age to talk to, to discuss things, not like the quiet, stoic Mr. Russell. He was given the job of showing Gerry how to operate various woodworking machines and the way they worked the benches, making joinery. The fact that he had someone to share his experience with, lifted his spirits no end, especially during lunch-hour. Gerry who lived near by preferred to have his lunch at work rather than rushing home, gobbling down a dinner and then rush back to work, all inside a half-hour. In no time they became good friends, helping each other when called upon to do so.

Gerry, was anxious to learn his trade, something they both had in common, meant that they got on well together. A few months after his arrival, Gerry was working on the surface planer, preparing parts for a new door, in the course of which he was pushing a three foot length of nine by two red deal timber on its flat, the lock rail of the door. He decided to change his position and move to the front of the machine, and started to pull the timber instead, with dire consequences. Without warning, the length of timber shot from his grasp and went flying down the workshop, striking the rear wall with a sharp thud. Gerry's hands dropped down on to the open blades of the machine, catching his hands. Blood sprayed everywhere, covering the machine. His cry for help alerted the others, who rushed to his assistance, first switching off the machine.

'Oh my God,' cried Mr. Russell, who blessed himself when he saw the amount of blood.

He would never forget as long as he lived, the shock on Gerry's face, as he wrapped his blood stained hand in his white apron. They feared the worst, the apron leaking more blood, only added to their anxiety. Gerry was escorted to the office, still in a state of shock, the ambulance was called for and they waited anxiously for it to arrive, and in no time he was safe in hospital.

He was given the unenviable task of cleaning down the bloody machine. It proved to be a gruesome task, nesscessitated taking the machine apart, cleaning it and then putting it together again, leaving the blood stained shavings to soak up the remains. Gerry was off work for a considerable amount of time, when he did eventually return to work, the damage to his right hand was serious. The tips of his three middle fingers had been sliced off, right to the bone, leaving him with a very tender hand.

'It could have been worse,' was his response, 'another few inches and it could have lost my hand'.

For someone who had just suffered such a terrible accident, his attitude was good and positive. It was going to take some time before his hand was restored to its former self, that's if it ever would. Needless to say, he was not asked to work that machine again! For each of them it proved a salutary lesson, a warning that machines can be very dangerous, great care had to be exercised, concentration had to be maintained all the time. Working a machine for a number of hours, can lead to tiredness, fatigue, one moment of carelessness sometimes results in a serious accident. It is not uncommon in joiner shops to see missing fingers and other forms of mutilations.

Came the day of joy, his father was coming home for good. No more two visits a year, summer and Christmas. With the ending of the terrible war in Europe, many fathers were returning home to their families. No more anxious times for wives, in many ways 'war-widows', who had waited through years of uncertainty, never knowing the day or the hour when they might become a widow. For the first time in ages, they were together as a family, not just two different units of one family. The effects were immediate and heart warming, especially for his mother, she became a different person, even laughing, something he thought she had forgotten.

At every possible opportunity they headed for the seaside, it did not matter which beach they went to, whatever bus came first, they headed for either Dollymount or Malahide.

That was the best time they ever had as a family, his parents were never so relaxed. His father even tried to teach them how to swim, with no great success, it was not very important, the sheer pleasure of just being together was sufficient.

It had been a difficult time for both parents, many marriages did not survive the trauma of enforced separation, The mother bringing up children as best she could, alone, a forerunner of to-day's single parents.

The men, working in factories and on building sites, living in camps, sleeping in the dreaded 'Nissen', huts, with severe rationing, food shortages and the ever present danger from enemy planes, especially at night, air-raid sirens going off at all hours of the night, only added to the uncertainty. It was years later that the full effects of these unhealthy conditions surfaced in the form of the deadly 'White Death', T.B*.

His father seldom made any reference to his days in England during the war, occasionally he would make some comment on the food they were obliged to eat. His face would display his absolute disgust at having to eat whale meat steaks or even worse, having to try and digest horse meat. His graphic discription of how hard it was to try and swallow, was stomach turning. To them, the very thought of eating a horse was appalling. He reserved his strongest criticism for what was called 'Spam', an evil tasting, factory made product, its contents defied discription. As for its taste, suffice to say, that it turned hard men into jelly at the very mention of its name. It was often suggested that it was invented by the German's as a secret weapon, designed to undermine the morale of the people, more powerful than a hundred bombs.

It certainly left its mark on those unfortunate enough who were forced to eat it. From time to time, he would mention what it was like during a air- raid, with bombs dropping all around, mostly when he had a few drinks on him, always wondering, if the next bomb was to be the last one, for you! Of the so-called 'hard chaws', who spent all their spare time and money, drinking and abusing themselves, and how they would be the first to drop on their knees to implore God's protection, to spare them, promising to amend their ways, at least until the next air-raid.

Ireland was in a depressed state, in spite of the fact that we were neutral, jobs were hard to find. The building trade was particularly bad; it was practically non-existent and the unemployment benefit money was only a subsistence. Somehow his father managed to find some work, mostly with small builders. The pay was just above the poverty line, but his mother was great with money, so they survived, but only just.

With the building trade in the doldrums, the future looked grim, his father took a chance and had some driving lessons to improve his chances of a job. The money to pay for the lessons was carefully saved, week after week, till the required amount was raised, not without great sacrifices on the part of his parents. His father got a whisper that C.I.E.* were recruiting staff for its Road Freight section, a driving licence was required, something few people had, he took the test and after much hoping and praying, he got the job, truck driving.

His mother was ecstatic,' Thank God, you are finished at the building game'. Father got the notice to start in Transport House in Bachelor's Walk. The fact that he had a regular job, made life more tolerable for all of them. The easing of food rationing was another factor that improved life for many people. He was thrilled when, sometimes his father would bring one of the trucks home at lunch-hour, for him it was great to sit behind the wheel of a big truck, imagining what it would be like to drive such a large truck. Naturally he was the envy of all his pals on the street, none of whose fathers drove a truck.

One of the first things his father made him do was to enrol in evening classes in Bolton Street Technical College to study for his trade certificates. At first he was not impressed with having to return to school. He thought that he was finished with school, but after the first few weeks he settled down to his studies and began to enjoy the challenge. The volume of work to be studied was considerable, with the practical work he had no problem, it was the theory that hurt the most.

Football was still an all consuming passion with himself and most of the gang, anything that might interfere with the weekly football match had to be eliminated. Smoking was an obvious non-starter, apart from the health risk, the cost saw to that. The same applied to drink, only more so, having managed to hold on to his Confirmation pledge of abstinence through his teens, (not that anyone ever heard of a teenager, you were a boy, then you became a man.) there was no way he was going to abandon it now, football was far to important.

Some time later he was playing for a local team, Celtic Park, when they were drawn at home to a team from the north county, St. Ita's, and they only managed to draw the quarter final match in the Dublin Amateur Cup. The re-match was arranged for the following Sunday in Portrane where St.Ita's were based. The referee had been told by the football association to get a result, regardless of what way the game went, the semi- finals were scheduled for the following week-end, and could not be re-arranged. After Mass, all eleven of them, plus a few others, piled into a van that belonged to one of the players' father and headed north to Portrane. It had been raining hard overnight with no sign of a let up. The football ground was situated in the grounds of the Mental Hospital, that overlooked the sea, a fine setting if the weather was kind. With the rain getting worse, they had to run from the van to the shelter of a wooden hut located in a corner of the pitch, that served as a dressing room. The pitch was like a pond, with water everywhere, all that was missing were a few ducks, who obviously had more sense than to be out on such a dreadful day.

To say that they were reluctant footballers was an understatement, even the referee had to force himself out of the comfort of the hut to get the game started. The home team changed into their football gear in the main building, where most of them worked as attendants or wardens, they were in no hurry to get the match started either. The referee finally conjured up enough courage to face the elements and made his way to the center of the waterlogged pitch, where he blew his whistle to summon the players. Somehow or other, a place in the semi-finals did not appear so attractive after all. Within one minute of leaving the dressing-room, they were all soaked to the skin and up to their ankles in mud and water. What followed was a complete farce, the very act of running was a joke and as for trying to kick the ball, a useless exercise. The leather football quickly became water-sodden and defied all efforts to propel it from one end of the pitch to the other. It remained bogged down in the center of the playing field, like a great, big, wet pudding. Most of his team paid little attention to their appearance, after all, it was only a football match, not a beauty contest. Not so for one member of the team, who always turned out immaculately dressed, ironed shorts with matching socks, even his football boots were polished. The look of distain on his face as he gently picked his step through a sea of mud, in a futile attempt to find a dry spot. As things turned out, he was one of the first to take a tumble, his spotless white gear disappeared, leaving him covered in muck from head to toe. Somehow or other, for the remainder of the game his heart did not seem to be in it, his appetite for football, like his lovely clean outfit, had disappeared.

With all of the players drenched, one's sympathy went to the unfortunate goalkeepers, having to stand 'like two stuffed dummies in the rain, at least the outfield players could move about and get the circulation going, not so for the goalkeepers. Half-time was reached without a score, not that it would have mattered, most of the players would have gladly settled for a toss of coin to decide the match. If anything, the weather deteriorated, with the wind driving in from the sea, drenching them with a cocktail of rain and sea water, adding to the already miserable conditions. No hot drinks were available at the interval, in fact, nothing but cold water to drink, something they had more than their fair share of. In an ideal situation, a change of gear would have been great, but like most teams at that time, they were lucky to have even one set of jerseys.

It was back to the mud and rain, with no respite, just more of the same. All concept of time and place was lost in the mud battle that followed. Coming near the end of normal time, the prospect of having to play extra time began to infiltrate the mind of each player, a daunting task. After a poor clearance by one of the St. Ita's players, the ball dropped at the feet of one of his team-mates, Jackie Brennan, who in sheer desperation had a swing at it and more out of luck than anything else, the ball sliddered across the mud and water, finishing up in the back of the net. The goalkeeper made no attempt at trying to stop it, he was probable as relieved as the rest of them to see an end to this farce, called a 'football' match. The end of the 'match' was greeted by a sigh of relief by both teams and the referee as they made their way to their respective dressing-rooms. The water soaked gear was dumped on the floor and wrung out as best as they could. Needless to say, there was no hot showers to ease the cold, just a rub down with a dry towel to help restore some sense of comfort. They had reached the semi-final, but no one felt like celebrating. It was only when they turned to make their way to the van, that for the first time, they noticed that the patients of the mental hospital were inside the building, dry and warm, looking out at the so-called 'sane' one's trying to play football in the rain. The irony was not lost on them.

CHAPTER 15

Radio Days

HIS introduction to radio was with a primitive crystal set he discovered hidden beneath the stairs in his grandparents house. A battered cardboard box covered with several layers of coal dust, coal had been stored there for many years, revealed a pair of ear phones, a probe and what appeared to be, a piece of coal. The coal was held in one hand, and the pointed probe searched for any radio station he could find, a real hit and miss affair, if by chance he managed to locate a station, no matter how faint, he held on for as long as possible. The war was over when he really became interested in radio proper, he was left with an abiding love of radio, a pleasure that is as strong as ever today. With the lifting of broadcasting restrictions, radio came into its own. It became more accessible to a wider audience, long before the intrusive advent of television.

B.B.C. Light programmes became the focal point for comedy, drama, entertainment and mercifully, no politics. Programmes like I.T.M.A. (It's That Man Again).with Tommy Hanley, Worker's Playtime, and the outrageous Goon's, were a must each week. The magnificent booming voice of ' The Man in Black', Valentine Dyall with his Mystery Playhouse every week that scared the living daylights out of many a young person, himself included. Vividly he recalled a radio adaptation of H.G.Well's 'War of the Worlds', with the redoubtable Professor Challenger saving the world, he had sat, transfixed to each episode, fascinated by the power of the story.

The magic of being permitted to stay up till three o'clock in the morning with his father listening to the commentary, direct from Madison Gardens, New York. of the heavyweight fight between the great Joe Louis and Jersey Joe Walcott, to think that the sound could travel that distance was indeed something out of this world.

The odd occasion he bothered to listen to Radio Éireann was for sport's results only. The station was perceived, rightly or wrongly as being dominated by a narrow minded clique of Irish speaking country people and G.A.A. fanatics. It may seem like a joke today but, Bing Crosby was banned from the air waves, his singing was considered decadent! Even more bizarre, was a priest who organised a campaign to have jazz outlawed from the radio, he referred to it as 'Devil's Music'. No official ban was imposed, but an unofficial one achieved the same result.

Around this time, Radio Luxembourg came on the scene, the forerunner of todays pop station's. with presenters Geoff Everett and Pete Murray, later to become disk jockeys. One of the most influential stations was A.F.N. (American Forces Network) serving the troops in Europe that played music direct from the U.S.A. One of the the most outrageous presenters was the 'Character' Fletcher as he discribed himself, and the music he played was great, with singers and bands of the highest order; Crosby, Sinatra, Mel Torme plus Peggy Lee, Jo Stafford and of course, Ella.

The hungry Fifties saw a revival of jazz, that offered a sense of lightness and freedom to the dark post war years. Even Radio Éireann responded with a 15. minute programme, hosted by a then little known, Gay Byrne. He got the bug, the jazz bug, radio became the medium through which he could indulge himself, long and short wavelength offered an unlimited feast of jazz, language was no barrier, the common thread was jazz.

His parents, to their eternal credit, never once objected to his high handed commandeering of the radio, notwithstanding the fact, that some of the music emanating from the radio set, was completely lost on them.

An old hand-cranked gramophone, borrowed from a friend of the family opened up a whole new world to him, records. This did present some difficulties, mostly financial. With a little ingenuity a way was found to overcome this problem. A shop in Wood Quay had a section containing hundreds of second-hand records, 78's of course, on display, all laid out in boxes, On some Sunday mornings, depending on the few bob available, a trip into town with his pals was the order of the day, the sense of anticipation while browsing through the records, in the hope of finding anything even remotely connected with jazz was sometimes rewarded. With no facilities to play the record, it was a case of pot luck, a real hit and miss affair. You paid your money one shilling and you took your chances, if the record turned out to be a dud, you could return later and sell it back for sixpence.

How could he ever forget finding a well worn copy of 'West End Blues'. recorded in 1928 by Louis Armstrong with the Hot Five, a classic recording, the opening cadenza when he soars to an 'E' above high 'C' and descends in a cascade of notes to a 'G' below middle 'C' has to be heard to be believed!

The music scene in Dublin began to improve, jazz concerts once a month in the Olympia Theatre with local musicians proved to be quite successful. At that time, a musicians strike in England prevented many of the great American bands playing there, and as a direct result, it was arranged for them to play in Dublin. Hundreds of fans made the hazardous journey by boat to attend each concert. Famous bands, like Stan Kenton, Woody Herman and the legendary Count Basie gave stunning performances in the Theatre Royal to packed houses.

It was while attending one of these concerts in the Olympia Theatre that an announcement was made to the effect, that the greatest of them all, Louis Armstrong, was to play here. In his wildest dreams he had never believed it was possible, to think that Louis was actually going to perform at the National Stadium in Dublin, a musical back water compared with London, was magic. He can still see the faces of his work mates, when they heard that he was going to pay £2.00. a ticket, just to hear music, he could well understand their surprise, as the weekly wage was around £8.00. What he had not mentioned was that he had purchased a ticket for both concerts, and it was worth every single penny.

Dean Oliver School of Modern Dancing

CHAPTER 16

Going Dancing

A group of them were sitting on a low wall beside the park contemplating what next, when one of the gang, Owen came out with a suggestion that startled the whole gang, and as a result things were never quite the same again.

'I think we should learn to dance.'

'You mean, dancing with girls? You must be joking,' replied Brian quickly.

'You'd hardly be dancing with boys,' answered Owen. 'I was talking with some of the fellas in work and they say there are some great bands in town.'

'Are you sure it's the bands you are interested in and not the girls?', retorted Brian, not showing much enthusiasm for the subject.

'Well if you go to a dance just to listen to the band, you would want your head examined,' replied Owen with a laugh.

'Where exactly would you go to learn to dance?', inquired Gerry quietly. That seemed to offer some encouragement to the idea.

'There's a place beside the 'Ranch',* near O'Connell Bridge, called Deane Oliver's. I believe it's a great place to learn,' said Owen, happy that he was getting through to some of them.

'It would cost a small fortune to go to a place like that,' said Brian, still not convinced.

'A half crown a lesson, one lesson a week, wouldn't break you,' snapped Owen, becoming a little impatient with the lack of interest being shown to his idea. 'For Jassus sake, I'll be nineteen next birthday and I have never been to a dance'.

'It's a big step for us. Ha I like that, a big step,' laughed Gerry, the joker in the pack.

'What are you talking about?,' answered Owen, feeling that he was losing the interest of the gang.

'You don't get it, do you? Dancing. A big step', repeated Gerry.

Someone reached over and pushed him off the wall, wherehe lay laughing to himself. 'You'se can't take a joke'.

'What about it, I say we give it a try, what have we to lose only a few bob?', insisted Owen.

'Not so fast, what will our parents say?,' asked Brian carefully. 'I can't see my oul fella letting me out dancing a few nights a week.'

'Look, you are like myself, just nineteen, surely there has to be more to life than football,' said Owen passionately. 'It's all very well for you'se that get a game every week, what about us, that never get a match?, you can't play football forever'.

'Right we'll take a vote on it. All in favour raise your hand?' suggested Brian. 'One, two, three, four, four with two against, what's next?'

'That's great,' answered a relieved Owen. 'I'll get the details in work. In the meantime, sound out your parents'

'Well, what did your parents say about the dancing?', inquired Owen, a few days later, anxious to hear what they were going to do.

'At first me da said, no way,' answered Joe,' but the Maasie worked on him for a few days and he finally agreed, on condition, that I be home before half ten.

'I'll be all right, me da is working in England', replied Dave, 'and me ma has no objections, although she looked a little sad when I mentioned dancing'.

'Maybe she is afraid of loosing her favourite son to another woman,' jeered Gerry.

'She would want to be hard up,' replied Joe with a laugh.

'Look who's talking, you're not exactly an oil painting yourself,' snapped Dave.

'Will you'se two cut out the messing', cried Owen. 'Are we going dancing or not?'

'What night is it on? I have to go to Tech two nights a week', he asked hopefully. 'Me da would have my life if I missed class'.

'Every Tuesday and Thursday', came the reply.

'That's great, I've no class on Tuesday', he said with a sigh.

'What about the rest of you, next Tuesday, can we all make it?', inquired Owen, half afraid to ask.

'Yes', came the answer he had been waiting for.

It was understandable that the parents were concerned for their family, they had a better knowledge of life. Certainly they had no wish to deprive them of the simple pleasure of dancing, at the same time, they had the responsibility as parents, something they took very seriously.

The following Tuesday evening the five of them, all spruced up in their best clothes, took the bus into town. One of the gang was missing, Peter, who said he had to work late but they found out later that his father had refused point blank to countenance anything to do with dancing. They found the place beside the Corinthian cinema, a narrow staircase led the way up two flights of stairs to a landing with the name 'Deane Oliver' suitably inscribed in faded gold lettering on a door that opened into a large room.

The walls were lined with chairs, girls on one side, boys on the other while four or five couples were dancing to the music of Victor Sylvester. They hesitated at the door. Even the bold Owen shrunk back, unsure, half afraid to enter.

'I don't think much of the music,' commented Joe, looking for an 'excuse to leave'.

'How could you listen to that rubbish music? I'm getting out of here,' said Brian, and with that he turned on his heels and charged down the stairs out on to the street, leaving the others to ponder their fate. They hesitated, trying to decide; one half wanted to stay, the other half happy to run. First one followed, then another and before they knew it, they were all out on the footpath debating between themselves, should they try again or forget the whole thing? They were so lacking in self confidence, that they could not make up their minds one way or the other. None of them had the nerve to go it alone.

'I say we try again,' said an impatient Owen.

'And I say we forget the whole thing and go to the pictures instead', replied Brian sharply.

'You'se can't spend the rest of your lives running away,' cried Owen, helplessly.

They just stood there for about ten minutes trying to reach a consensus. In the end, Owen retorted out loud.' Shag you'se anyway, I'm going up again and I don't care who follows'.

'I say we take another vote,' suggested Gerry tentatively.

'For Jassus sake, you are the greatest bunch of chickens I ever seen,' answered Owen angrily, and with that, he headed back up the stairs leaving the others in a state of total confusion. Looking at each other and still undecided, without as much as a word, they almost got caught in the door as they fell up the stairs after Owen, all looking rather sheepishly at each other.

After paying the fee they were welcomed by a tall, elegant lady who walked like she had springs in her shoes. She wore a long black dress and spoke with a very swanky accent as she led the way into the other room. at the rear of the building.

'First allow me to welcome you all to the Deane Oliver School of Modern Dancing. I will be your instructor. My function is to teach the basic steps, I will be showing you how to dance the Slow Waltz, the Foxtrot and the Quick Step, in that order. Depending on your progress, you can advance to more complicated routines. We will commence by forming a line, facing the wall'.

There were ten other fellas like themselves trying to look as incospicuous as possible, keeping as far as they could from the instructor, so as not to look stupid when the class commenced.

'Come along now, form a line, feet together, arms by your side, and right foot forward. I said right foot'.

Half of the class put their left foot forward. There was much shuffling of feet as they tried to adjust to the correct position.

'Bring your left foot forward and sideways, feet together. I will demonstrate for you again. Now pay attention! Right foot forward, left foot forward, feet together. That was not too difficult'.

'This dancing is a piece of cake,' said Gerry, as they returned to their seats.

'That's what you think, wait till you have to make a turn,' replied Joe, who had some difficulty trying to decide which foot was left or right.

'I am looking for a volunteer to demonstrate what we have learned so far,' said the instructor, looking across the floor, after they had been going backwards and forwards for a half an hour or more. On hearing this request, they all shrunk to the back of the room trying to become invisible.

'That young man with the fair hair,' called the instructor, 'you can be first'.

'Who, me?,' asked a shocked Joe, looking around for support, only to find himself alone. The others had forsaken him, thankful he had been chosen and not one of them. He was panic stricken.

Yes, you! Come here, we will show how much we have learned,' she said cheerfully.

Joe froze, unable to move, looking for support but none was forthcoming, the others were quite happy it was him and not them. Sympathy they had for him but that was all. The instructor bounded across the floor and to his horror, she grabbed him around the waist and pulled him close to her. The look on his face had to be seen to be believed and with one step they were on the floor. She swept him off his feet, but in spite of her best efforts, he made every mistake possible even managing to walk on her feet. When finished, he staggered across the floor and collapsed on to the chair saying,' this is the last time I'm coming here'.

'Thank God it was you and not me,' said a nervous Owen. Perhaps it had not been such a good idea after all.

'I only hope you get caught the next time,' retorted a very angry Joe, convinced that he had made a complete fool of himself. 'It's all your fault we are here in the first place.'

'I'd have died if she asked me too dance,' said Brian not looking too brave.

They spent the next hour going backwards and forward, making many mistakes but in the end making some progress before collecting their coats and out on to the street, a very sober and quiet bunch of young men, each with their own thoughts.

'That wasn't so bad after all,' said a cheerful Owen.' Whose's coming back next week?'

'Why not, it was a laugh. I never saw so many left-footed people in my life before', replied Brian.

'You weren't exactly Fred Astaire yourself', he stated with a grin.

'Even if I say so myself, I thought I handled my self rather well this evening,' answered Gerry, puffing out his chest and running his hand through his short curly hair.

'Are you kidding, you were like an elephant on hot bricks,' snapped Joe, still smarting from his ordeal with the instructor.

'You should talk, more like Gene Kelly with two broken legs,' replied a happy Owen. 'Let's head for Cafolla's and celebrate, to hell with the cost'.

'Are you buying?, he asked quickly.

'I'd like my job, throwing ice cream into you lot,' replied Owen. He was walking on air and he had every right to be, it had been his idea in the first place.

They crossed O'Connell Street to the ice cream parlour, all feeling great. Their first tentative step into the adult world, had been a valuable experience, but no one was prepared to say out loud. To express any feelings, especially on such a sensitive subject as girls was not on. You kept those feelings to yourself, you suppressed anything that might be interpreted as having an interest in the opposite sex.

Just to prove how good they felt, they each ordered a 'Melancholy Baby' and indulged themselves. Not for a moment would any of them suggest going to a pub, most of them were still teetotal Pioneers. Anyhow for them football was total, anything that might interfere with the playing football was out of the question.

Over the following weeks, slowly, ever so slowly, they progressed through each dance to the quick-step, but not without some very red faces. The trauma of having to demonstrate in front of the class with the lively instructor, left each of them weak at the knees. After four weeks trying to learn, they were promoted to the improver's class, which meant mixing with girls, who were doing a similar course in another room. The first time they danced with the girls was indeed difficult for both boys and girls. It was impossible to say which were the most embarrassed, as tentatively they ventured forth, scared stiff of making fools of themselves. The very fact of holding a girl in a dancing position induced much confusion and embarrassment for the boys. All those steps, so carefully learned over the weeks were forgotten, standing on the partners feet, was followed by profuse apologies, swearing never to set foot inside this place again, was the order of the day. It was probably the same for the girls, but how were they to know, they had to just, grin and bear it, and hope the next time things would improve. Adding to the dilemma, the lady instructor would, in her wisdom intervene if as she saw it, you were making a mistake, telling the boy to put his arm around the girl's waist and pull her close, saying, 'that you cannot dance properly at arms length'.

There were many red and perspiring faces among the boys as they tried to make some sense of the dancing. The slow-waltz and the fox-trot were favourites, the quick-step was the cause of great concern, trying to remember the sequence of steps at speed was a major problem for both boys and girls.

'No more Deane Oliver's for me,' announced Owen to the gang, after another session of dancing! That's all finished'.

'Do you hear your man?,' he interrupted with a laugh, 'only a few weeks ago you didn't know your left foot from your right. Me thinks it's not the dancing he's after. Did you see the one he was dancing with last night?'

'What are you talking about?, answered Owen, a little too quickly,' she knows a good dancer when she sees one.'

'She must be hard up', replied Gerry. 'Fancy your chances with her, do you?'

'I don't know what you are talking about,' said an embarrassed Owen, his face turning a bright shade of red.

Fate took a hand, in the form of two tickets given to Gerry by one of his work mates for a dance in the Crystal ballroom in Annes Street. By buying six tickets, they got two free ones, so they divided the cost between them and took the plunge.

'I'll have to get me parents permission to stay out late,' stated Joe. 'I'm not sure if they will let me'.

'For Jassus sake, grow up will you'. retorted Owen.' You're nearly twenty years of age, you' ll be out of your time next year'

'Just the same, I'll have to get the O.K. from me da', replied Joe nervously, not enamoured with the idea.

By the end of the week, all had received the all clear, except Joe, whose father had refused point blank to even consider such a liberty. Without as much as a word of regret, Joe accepted, respecting his father's decision, his own feelings suppressed. 'Maybe the next time'.

This caused some of the others to hesitate. Feelings of guilt, intermingled with frustration. They had all been pals for years, played football together, and the loss of one of the gang was felt by each of them. It undermined what little confidence they shared with each other, a confidence that depended on the gang holding together.

It was something to witness that Saturday night, each arrived in his Sunday best, with plenty of good natured slagging taking place, but in a nervous self-conscious way. At the entrance they were carefully scrutinised by the 'bouncers', to see if their dress conformed with the code of the place a suit with collar and tie.

'Remember, no jiving, or lurching, or you are out on your ear, and no refund either', warned the 'bouncer', a bruiser of a man, complete with cauliflower ears and a flat nose.

This being their first outing they arrived shortly after eight o'clock to find themselves virtually alone in the spacious ballroom, with only a handful of people dotted about the place. Finding a quiet corner, they patiently waited for the crowd to arrive, while the band played away, regardless of whether people danced or not. They were paid to play for four hours, if nobody danced, so be it. A few couples, took advantage of the empty floor to demonstrate their dancing skills. The boys watched and admired the precision and timing of the dancers, only too well aware of their own shortcomings.

'What if they all dance like that?', inquired a not so brave Owen. 'We would make right fool of ourselves'.

'Speak for yourself', answered Dave, with an air of confidence. 'It's a piece of cake'.

'Do you hear your man talking?,' rounded Owen. 'I don't see you falling over yourself getting up to dance'.

'When the time is right, just you wait and see', replied Dave with a smile.

After what seemed like ages, the hall began to fill up. Still none of them ventured forth. The first step would be the hardest. They just sat there, too scared to move. Finally in desperation, Owen plucked up all the courage he could muster, and walked across the dance floor to one of the girls with the intention of asking for a dance. Before he could ask the girl she was whisked away into the now crowded floor by another young man, leaving Owen standing like a fool in the centre of the floor. He quickly scurried back to the safety of the gang, his face red with embarrassment.

'Hard luck, Owen, better luck the next time,' said Gerry quietly, not wishing to make things any worse.

'It's easy for you', snapped Owen, 'sitting there on your arse. If you are so brave, why don't you have a go?' Gerry did not reply, he was conscious how Owen felt, he had no desire to add to his pal's troubles.

The uneasy silence was broken by an announcement that saw many of the men making themselves scarce, to avoid the dreaded 'Ladies Choice'. It was perceived by some of them as an afront to their masculinity, being forced to dance with some of the less than glamorous girls, however a refusal to dance could mean ejection by one of the 'bouncers'.

One by one they were picked off by the girls to dance and all those weeks of slow slow-quick-slow amounted to nothing. What they had so diligently struggled to learn, the forward steps, sideways and backwards turned out to be useless. All that was required was to shuffle around the over crowded dance floor, trying not to step on the girl's feet. It proved to be quite an ordeal but somehow they managed to survive without causing too much damage to their dancing partners. It was a start. The dance was returned and in no time at all they were very happy to shuffle around the dance floor. The interval arrived, and collecting a return pass at the door, they cheerfully headed for an ice cream parlour in Grafton Street.

On their return, with each dance their confidence grew, easily adjusting their footwork to the crowded floor. With the pubs closing at ten thirty it was only possible to edge shoulder to shoulder around the floor. The clock reminded them that it was time to go, so getting their coats from the cloakroom, they walked to the bus stop in Grafton Street just in time to see their bus go breezing by and not stopping.

With panic they raced after the speeding bus, hoping to intercept it at the next stop. They turned the corner of Suffock Street in time to see the bus pull away from the bus stop, forcing them to charge straight ahead on to College Green in a desperate attempt to stop the bus. The bus nosed its way round by the bank into Westmoreland Street chased by the now frantic gang. All thoughts of dancing were forgotten in the mad rush get on the bus. If they failed to catch the bus, not only was there a long walk home, but it jeopardised any hopes they might have of going dancing in the near future. They were saved by the crowd of passengers that delayed the bus long enough for them to scramble aboard, breathless, before the conductor declared. 'Standing room only – sorry, Missus, but the bus is full'.

Come Lent all dancing came to a halt, as was the law. Every dance hall in the country closed dawn for the holy season of Lent. With it went the jobs of those who worked there, including the musicians, who faced seven weeks of unemployment. They had no choice but to take the boat to England and try and find some work. Mostly they found work in the Irish clubs, living hand to mouth, with very poor travel and living conditions to contend with. With the approach of Easter, it was back across the Irish sea, to be ready for the re-opening of the dance halls on Easter Monday.

With dancing not available, except for football, the cinema was the only place for entertainment and as none of the gang drank, the pub was no place for aspiring footballers. Even the cinema's closed for Holy Week, ostensibly for re-decorating, but most people knew that it came under the persuasive influence of the Catholic Church.

Apart from football, the only other sport they had an interest in was, snooker, particularly during the long winter evenings. Alcohol had not yet raised it's ugly head. At the top on Hollybank Road was 'Jack's Snooker Hall,' with about twelve tables and of course, two or three pin-ball tables, to soak up any loose change that was available. It was a handy place to go on a cold winters evening when funds were low, with six of them playing each game, the cost did not amount too much. Money or no money, there was always a game in progress, especially on table No.1. where all the 'hot-shots' played. Just to sit and watch them play was a treat. The skill and precision, as they seemed to be able to pot any ball at will, was to them, amazing. Himself and his pals, aspired to one day, play on table No.1. That was the height of their ambition. No matter how often or how hard they tried, it alluded them.

They tried, oh how they tried, coming close to what was considered an acceptable level of incompetence. Just when it seemed that they were up to the standard required, the place burned down, thus ending any hopes they might have had of ever playing on table No.1.

At the Metropole.

CHAPTER 17

Dress Dance

THE inevitable arrived in the form of an invitation by one of the gang to attend a dress dance being organised by the company he worked for. Greeted with dismay by some, welcomed by others, the division was equal. It induced much soul searching, as each of them wrestled with another phase in their development.

'Where in God's name are we going to get a partner from?', was the question on everyone's lips. None of them had ever been on a date, the prospect of having to invite a girl to a dress dance, was daunting

'What about your sister?,' asked Gerry, half joking, whole in earnest.

'My sister, are you kidding?,' replied Joe. 'She wouldn't be caught dead with the likes of you.'

'Thanks a lot, you're a great help' answered Gerry, taking offence from the reply he had received.

'I didn't mean to insult you,' replied Joe,' but she is only a kid and won't be sixteen 'til next August'.

'Baby snatcher, that's what you will be called,' interjected Sean.

'I don't care if she is in pig tails, as long as she looks the part', came the answer from Gerry, with a note of desperation in his voice.

'I'll ask her, not that it will make much difference', replied Joe. 'Me ma would have kittens at the prospect of her darling daughter going dancing'.

'Jassus, what am I going to do? The dance is next week', cried a very unhappy Gerry. The fact that it was he who introduced the notion of a dress dance to the gang, did not sit too well. Apart from the gang, the fellas he worked with would give him a hard time if he failed to show up on the night which only added to his misery'

It was much the same for each of them, with various degrees of success. The stress was enormous for those who had so far failed to find a partner. As the fateful day edged closer, it did nothing for their fragile confidence. There was also the not inconsiderable matter of the finance, with tickets paid for in advance and no refund for anyone who did not turn up on the night, only added to their perilous state of mind. Desperation, allied with the constant pressure from their mates to find someone, even one with a wooden leg, was becoming unbearable. Two of them managed to swap sisters, which received the approval of their parents. Another, somehow persuaded one of the girls attached to his scout troop to accompany him, but not without first sweating blood, before conjuring up the courage to ask her.

She responded immediately, almost as if she had been waiting for the invitation, that this was to be her first dress dance too. The word had spread on the grapevine to all the local talent that the boys were on the look out for prospective dancing partners. Sheepish smiles were extended by some of the girls in the direction of the boys, not that they noticed, they were totally oblivious to such subtilities. For those fortunate enough to find a suitable partner, the next stage was the hiring of a dress suit, a Monkey Suit as it was commonly known.

'You better go and knock on the door and ask,' said Joe firmly to Sean, who had so far failed to find someone to invite to the dance.

'Do you realise what you are asking me to do?,' cried a nervous Seán, who was at his wit's end.

'It's your problem, not mine. I'm only trying to help', answered Joe. 'The dance is in a few days, and you're running out of time'.

Sean was the last of the gang without a partner. He fancied a girl who lived down the road, and had done for a while, but only from a distance. Whatever about approaching her, there was no way he could ask her to a dance.

'I'll come with you to offer moral support', said Joe, trying to reassure his mate.

So down the road the pair of them marched, but as they approached the house Sean began to chicken out. Joe had to literally push him in the gate and stood waiting till Seán knocked on the door. Seán's heart was going berserk inside his shirt, his mouth had dried up, with his tongue like a piece of sandpaper as he waited for the door to open. Perhaps no one was home so he was wasting his time. Better to suffer the loss of the tickets, as it was hardly worth all the stress. So he might get some slagging from his pals, but he could live with that.

His thoughts were interrupted by the opening of the door. A large formidable lady filled the door opening, her appearance only heightened his anxiety, he almost collapsed with fear.

'Excuse me ma'am, but is Mary home?,' he muttered through his dry mouth, with a sigh that came from the soles of his feet.

'Please come in, I'll get her for you', as she turned and headed for a four panel door at the end of a long, narrow hall, leaving him to ponder his fate. What next?. Another door. half way down the hall was open to reveal a small parlour crowded with heavy furniture. Half daring to look in case he was caught doing so, he could not help but admire the comfortable room, a far cry from his own humble one room flat. The opening of the door, reminded him of his mission, as Mary walked towards him, smiling brightly.

'Well Seán, good to see you,' she said quietly, 'come into the parlour please.'

He followed her, with the smell of camphor filling the room. They sat opposite each other, him with a thin nervous smile. He had never, ever spoken to her before and it scared him. Neither of them spoke, they just sat there staring at each other, the silence was deafening.

'Did you want to see me about something?,' she asked, breaking the silence.

'Yes', he replied quickly, a little too quick.

'Well, what is it?,' her response seemed to hint at impatience.

'I was wondering if you would like to come to a dress dance with me', he blurted out, his face the colour of fresh beetroot.

'When is it?', she inquired.

'Next Friday, in the Metropole', he answered, 'all the gang are going'.

'I'd love to go but there's not much time to get a dress,' she replied graciously. 'I will have to get my parents permission. Excuse me and I will go and ask them'.

With that she left the room, gently closing the door behind her. He leaned back in the soft armchair, all was not lost, not yet anyway, he had at least tried. It was now in the lap of the gods. Abruptly the door was opened by the mother, closely followed by Mary, he jumped to his feet and at the same time tried to read her face, but it revealed nothing.

'So you wish to take our Mary to a dress dance?' she asked politely.

'Yes, ma'am,' he replied nervously.

'You do realise, that Mary has never been to anything like this before', stated the mother.

'Neither have I, ma'am', he answered.

'How may I ask, are you going to the dance?, inquired the mother,' and more important, how do you propose to get home after'?.

'The whole gang are going together on the bus and we are sharing a taxi after,' he replied. Maybe there was a chance after all.

'Will there be any drinking at this affair?', the mother asked firmly. Mary stood there without making a sound, giving nothing away.

'No ma'am, definitely not, we are all Pioneers', he lied.

'I hope not. Having discussed it with Mary's father, we agree, with one condition, that Mary be home before midnight at the latest,' came the reply though he doubted if Mary's father had much say in the decision.

'That's great, I have to be in work the next day, so I don't need a late night either', answered a relieved Sean.

'Good, I'll leave you both to make whatever arrangements you have to make'. We will see you on Friday', and with that she left the room.

'Thank you very much ma'am,' happy to see the back of her. Turning to Mary he said. 'I hope you didn't mind me asking you'.

'Not at all, as a matter of fact, I was half hoping you would', she replied graciously, 'it's the talk of the road'.

'Then I'll see you on Friday, about seven', he suggested.

'I'll be ready, and thanks for asking me', she responded.

Once outside, although his knees were still knocking, he skipped down the road to where Joe was patiently waiting.

'Well, how did you get on?,' inquired Joe, anxious to hear what the result was.

'No problem, had them eating out of the palm of my hand', he lied again.

'Half expected you to be turfed out on your ear', replied Joe, happy to know that everything had, so far gone according to plan. At the same time, he knew full well that it was only an act designed to conceal the real truth.

The day drew ever so close. Mother's had to work late into the night preparing the fancy dresses, sewing machines buzzed away, with much time devoted to fitting and refitting. Tons of pins were called into play, then discarded, before all was ready for the big day.

Joe left work early to collect the dress suit before they closed, and to purchase the mandatory box of chocolates. He had asked his mother to get some flowers for him, not wishing to be seen with a bouquet of flowers. If anyone saw him, he would never live it down. Then washed, shaved, clean shirt, the monkey suit, complete with bow tie and armed with the chocolates and flowers, first checking that it was dark outside, one could not be to careful, especially with flowers, he made his way to the girl's house. Both his parents wished him good luck, his dad slipped him a few pounds as just in case money, and waved goodbye. Down the street he strutted on his first date, trying to hide the flowers beneath his coat. They had arranged for all to meet in Michael's house, before taking the bus into town. With time to spare, he was on the lookout for any of the gang, not a soul in sight, must be too early for them, when he reached the girl's house.

There was not a sign of life about the house, so he gave the bell a long ring and waited. The click of a switch brought a flood of light to the hall. The clear outline of a figure materialised behind the glass panel door. He checked his tie and ran his fingers through his hair and was ready. When the door opened, he just stood there with the flowers in one hand and the chocolates in the other, a stupid grin on his pimply face, he felt like a real 'Wally'. The look on Kathleen's face told him something was amiss, perhaps her dress was not ready or her parents had changed their mind about letting her go to the dance. He could read trouble in her eyes. She was dressed in everyday clothes, no fancy dress, no fancy hair style. She began to laugh, quietly at first, and then just stood there in fits of laughter.

'Where in the name of the blessed God are you going, dressed like that?', she asked, with tears streaming down her face.

'To a dress dance, where else?', he replied, still at a loss to understand why she was not ready. 'We have to meet the gang in half an hour'.

'You don't get it, do you?,' answered Kathleen, still smiling brightly.

'Get what?,' he replied, at a loss to know what was going on.

'The dance is not till tomorrow night', she said as graciously as she could, not wishing to hurt his feelings.

'Tomorrow, but the tickets say the 27th, that's today', he responded, as his stomach began to turn slowly.

'Today is the 26th,' she giggled, almost in a state of collapse, trying to hold back the tears.

'You mean, I am a day too soon', he gulped, as the penny began to drop. He felt like a real eejit. How was he ever going to live it down?. He started to perspire with embarrassment, the collar of his new shirt felt stiff and tight, it was choking him to death, he wished it would. They stood there looking at each other, one in a convulsion of laughter, the other ready to die.

'I'll see you tomorrow,' he muttered in a confused state of mind, 'You better keep these,' handing her the flowers.

'Thanks very much, you shouldn't have bothered, really', she answered seriously, not wishing to add to his discomfort. 'See you tomorrow'.

He got out the gate as quickly as he could, wanting to get as far as possible on this the worst day of his life. His ears were steaming hot, someone was talking about him, and he knew exactly what they were saying. There was also the not inconsiderable matter of having to pay for a second day's hire of the dress suit.

The next night they crowded into the small house, the girls bedecked in their finest. This was the first time since confirmation to have an opportunity to do so, all coy and giggles, a fitting tribute to their respective mother's hard work. There was no competition between them, it was all so new and exciting. After the introductions had been made, though they all sort of knew each other anyway, the girls were shepherded into the parlour, which had taken on the appearance of a mini 'Botanic Garden'. with flowers everywhere, to say nothing of chocolates. The boys took refuge in the living room with a great deal of slagging of each others appearance. Time to leave, so down the road they marched in pairs, causing quite a stir to people on the road, not accustomed to such a display of style.

They crowded round the bus stop, all laughs and jokes, it was great to be young, on the threshold of life, and with the arrival of the bus, they commandeered the front seats with the approval of the conductor and passengers, who were happy to share in their experience. It lent some colour to an otherwise ordinary bus ride. Likewise, in O'Connell Street they were afforded a similar reception, even the endless traffic relented, allowing them to cross unhindered to the brightly lit Metropole.

'Which floor is the dress dance on please?' Sean asked the uniformed Commissioner who had opened the door for them.

'2nd floor, Sir,' came the reply.

'What do you think, girls, should we take the lift?' asked Gerry. The stairs would be very awkward in those long dresses'.

'The lift it is,' they all agreed

It proved to be a tight squeeze, what with the fluffy dresses and all, but they somehow managed to cram in. The lift staggered to rise, it was certainly overloaded, well above the permitted weight, but they survived. Not that anyone noticed in the excitement of their first real dance, breaking out for the first time. The trestle gates slid open and they all piled out, making lots of noise in the process. The place was crowded with like minded young people, similarly dressed and just as excited.

'Can you see our table?' inquired Gerry, searching the large room, trying to locate their table.

'It's over here,' replied Sean, pointing to a table near the wall.

There was much confusion when it came to the seating arrangements, with everyone trying too hard to be polite with each other. The girls finally taking the initiative and sorting out the places. The boys, sheepishly backed off, not knowing what to do, happy to let the girls decide. It was amusing to observe the antics of the boys, as they tried to mimic scenes from the cinema, where the gent placed the chair for the ladies to sit down.

The girls, for their part, revelled in the attention being paid them and responded graciously. The meal, when served, presented more problems for some of them, unaccustomed to such a lavish display of cutlery. Which spoon for the soup? Which knife for bread? Even the different glasses only added to the confusion. Lemonade and soft drinks were the order of the table, some of the boys fancied something more stimulating, but refrained, for the moment anyway, out of respect for the girls.

No one made a move to eat. They watched each other and waited, till Gerry grabbed a spoon and commenced eating the soup, when it was discreetly pointed out to him that he was using the wrong spoon.

'If I am wrong, then so are half of the people in this room,' and he was right.

After enjoying a fine meal, even if some of them were still a little up tight, the music and dancing soon broke down any remaining barriers that existed. Some of the more adventurous boys had been observed sneaking out to the bar to indulge in something stronger than lemonade. It certainly changed their behaviour and they really let themselves go.

Michael of all people, a quiet sort of guy, could not stop talking, mostly silly talk, making stupid jokes and laughing out loud, much to the discomfort of his partner, Eileen. Any attempt to quieten him down was met with more outrageous behaviour, leaving the girl mortified. He would jump up and insist on dancing with other girls, he would then proceed to charge around the dance floor, bumping into other dancers, making a proper nuisance of himself. So much so, that one of the bouncers, a giant of a man, with all the hallmarks of a former boxer, quietly, but firmly, escorted him to his seat.

'You just sit there and enjoy the rest of the evening, Sir', was all he said, but it was the way he said it, that meant only one thing – behave or else.

Mary and Sean got off to a shaky start, both were almost afraid to speak to each other, Sean's experience in her house did nothing for his confidence. If anything, it had weakened it. Of the two Mary showed a greater tendency to communicate while he remained tongue-tied. Even then, it was a slow, painful awakening.

Once they started dancing he opened up like an oyster, and he couldn't stop talking. Mary, to her credit, let him ramble on, interjecting from time to time to express her views. As they were fairly good dancers, this only helped to make the evening a success for both of them. With the excitement of the evening, no one bothered with the time, till the band leader announced the last dance, creating panic, particularly for the girls, with the realisation that it was 1.30.a.m. and they had been warned to be home before midnight or face the consequences. Mary and Sean dived into the first taxi that came the road, quickly followed by Kathleen and Gerry, who had sobered up. They urged the driver to put his foot down, saying it was a matter of life and death, maybe it was.

It was a chastened pair that rolled out of the taxi, Sean ushered Mary in the gate without making a sound. When they reached the hall door, Mary was reluctant to knock, fearing the worst. She had visions of her parents reaction to such a late hour and their dismissal of Sean for his part in her downfall. Sean, for his part, was just as fearful, they had enjoyed such a great evening, pity it had to end on such a low note.

'I'll see you during the week,' he said quietly. 'The photos should be ready in a few days'.

'Thanks Sean, I had a really wonderful time,' she replied, 'see you later'.

In a moment of madness, he reached over and gave her a 'Gooser'* on the cheek. Before she could react, he was gone.

Crusaders F.C. under 17. team in 1950

CHAPTER 18

On the Move Again

ABOUT this time, they were awarded a Corporation house in Ballyfermot, a million miles from where they lived. It was good bye to their pals again, having built up a wide circle of friends. They were transported to a new housing estate, not knowing a soul. It also meant he had to cycle to the North Strand and back every day, a considerable distance, especially in winter. Likewise for his brother Noel, who had got an apprenticeship at the poultry trade, in Donnybrook, another 'Chicken Choker' in the family. It was not as far as North Strand but it was no mean feat just the same, after a day's work.

One of the problems with new housing estates is the lack of basic services, not even a Church had been provided. Removed from their pals, he found the isolation hard to deal with. Making a few return trips to Drumcondra, only made things worse. While attending Mass in Adam and Eve Church, Merchants Quay, he discovered that they had a lending library. He lost no time in getting himself a library ticket. It turned out to be quite a good library, with many fine books. What he found rather strange was that each book had been censored, with a line drawn through any word or sentence that might be discribed as 'offensive'. Some words scribbled out were legible and were, to say the least, quite trivial. With the censorship laws in place at that time, it was hardly necessary to re-censor any book. It being a Church library, he well understood. Nonetheless, it must have taken a great deal of time and patience to go through each and every word and sentence in search of, what can only be discribed as harmless words.

His father had transferred to driving a bus and was now based in Conygham Road depot, not far from their new home which gave him regular hours and meals. One of the redeeming features of the new house was that he got to have room to himself, a real luxury indeed, after all those years in one room. His parents had the large front bedroom and his two brothers had to share the other bedroom. Life was good, with three of them bringing in wages especially for his mother, for the first time in her life did not have to count every penny. There was even talk of a family holiday, something unheard of in those days. The furthest his parents got was to Fairyhouse races one Easter Monday.

His father, who had smoked most of his life, developed a terrible cough that racked his whole body and after much persuasion by his mother, he reluctantly agreed to go and see a doctor. The usual tests were carried out, including X-rays, before he was diagnosed as having T.B. The dreaded 'White Death' as it was commenly known, that had ravaged thousands of families, filled graveyards in every county. In no time, his father was moved to St. Mary's sanatorium situated in the Phoenix Park. Each of the family was subjected to a rigorous health check to see if the infection had spread. It was several anxious weeks before the results were confirmed, which thankfully, proved negative. For a short few years, they had enjoyed a moment of 'prosperity', now it was a return to the hard times, apprentice wages did not amount to much.

During all this trauma, his poor father never complained, he just accepted his fate stoically. Being confined to bed was probably the worst thing he was obliged to endure. For one who had spent all his working life out doors, it could not have been easy for him, those dreadful war years had taken their toll.

So began for him, years of hospitalisation, culminating in the 'Rib' operation, where a number of ribs were removed and also the affected part of his lung. The setting for St. Mary's was magnificent, surrounded by many fine mature trees, with a long winding driveway. It nevertheless meant little to those visiting patients in the hospital. It was a return to tight management, of which his mother was an expert. The sick benefit did not amount to much. They were never short of food or clothing but there was little else. Twice a week the family headed for St. Mary's armed with whatever bits and pieces they could afford, they looked forward to the visits, although there was very little to do but try and make the visit as interesting as possible for their father. It must have been a long day for him, just lying there, looking out the window, with only visits from his family to brighten up an otherwise miserable day. How he managed to put in his time, we will never know. Some attempt was made to relieve the boredom by doing hand craft, making lamp shades, sewing boxes, things like that but it only served to underline the monotony of hospital life.

Apart from the enforced confinement, there was the dark shadow of T.B. hanging over him. Over a period of time, other patients in the same ward would go missing, to be replaced by new arrivals. No one asked what had become of the missing patients, they all knew, but were afraid to ask.

For his mother, once again trying to rear three young men on her own, life had not been kind to her, there were few pleasures, while a social life was non-existent. Fortunately, not far from their home, in the local de -la- Salle school, someone had the foresight to show films a few nights a week. It proved to be very popular indeed, especially in a new housing estate, where there was no outlet at all for people. A journey into town was not very practical, what with bus fares and the time taken to travel. It was welcome relief for his mother, who loved the pictures, so each of them in their turn accompanied her, depending on the film showing. The seats were not exactly cushy or very comfortable but that was of little consequence, it was an escape from the harsh reality of life.

Life still had its lighter moments; his younger brother, Pat and one of his pals, Michael, were crossing an open space close to their home, that had recently been vacated by builders, who had moved to another part of the site. Suddenly, without warning, Michael disappeared into a hole in the ground, right up to his arm pits. He was so shocked that he could not even cry out. His face was a mixture of pain and horror, and at a loss to know what had happened to him. Pat just as shocked, jumped back fearing for his own safety.

'Help me', cried a desperate Michael, having regained his breath.

Gingerly Pat approached, testing the ground with his foot, making sure it was safe. Satisfied that there was no danger he reached down and attempted to pull Michael out of the hole in the ground. Getting a firm grip with his hand, he started to drag as hard as he could. Slowly he emerged from the hole, slipping and sliding to his feet. He stood there still trying to take in what had befallen him. He was covered with the most foul, evil, disgusting slime right up to his neck, the most obscene sight imaginable, with the appearance of a creature that had crawled out of a swamp, and the smell, a sickening, overpowering, stench filled the quiet morning air. Pat was appalled with what he had just witnessed, not sure which was the worst, the slime or the obnoxious smell.

Telling Michael not to move, as if he could, he ran as fast as he could to tell his mother what had happened to her son. At first she thought he was joking, things like that don't really happen, but at Pat's insistence she brought with her an old sheet, just in case. When she saw the state of her son she almost wept. Even to approach him required all her self control, not wishing to add to his awful predicament. The smell seemed to have increased in intensity. To wrap the sheet around him was nearly more than she was capable of, but somehow she managed.

The poor boy slugged his pitiful way home, with his mother's assistance, the squelching of his shoes only added to his discomfort, while Pat followed at a safe distance. Once home, he was stripped naked and stood over a yard gully, while his mother tried her best to clean him down. Buckets of hot water, disinfectants, soaps anything to try and remove all traces of the slime that covered him. When he was considered reasonably clean, he was then allowed take a bath, with more of the same cleaning agents, before he was given clean clothing. The remains of his soiled clothes were dumped in the dust bin.

It later emerged that he had fallen into a cess-pool, the remains of a 'temporary' latrine erected by builders. A galvanised iron partition was put in place, a hole was dug in the ground with a single plank, supported by a few concrete blocks, and acted as the seat. Before the builders left the site, the hole was back-filled, in this case sufficient cover had not been provided. One wonders if the 'hole' had been deeper, the outcome could have been more tragic. He was later to experience for himself similar working conditions.

About this time, his apprenticeship was complete and he was working as a jobbing carpenter for various builders in the city, finding work when it became available but at times it was scarce.

The weekly visits to his father continued for many months and it extended into years but and still no sign of his release. All the while, he continued to play football, on several occasions he played in the 15 acres in the Phoenix Park, right in the shadow of St. Mary's sanatorium. It was almost obscene for him to be playing football, and at the same time his father was stretched out in a hospital bed fighting for his very life. It would never occur to them not to come and see him. You went to visit your father, not out of a sense of duty, but because he was your father, it was as simple as that.

After what seemed a life time, he was released and he came home, a tall, gaunt figure of a man. He appeared even taller than they remembered him, the operation having been a success, but it had taken it's toll, never other than thin, he looked like a refugee from Belsen prison camp.

Then followed months of recuperation, as he sought to rebuild his health, he was tough, and before the end of the year, he was passed fit to return to work, naturally, he stopped smoking.

About this time, his Gran McHugh had passed away peacefully in St. James hospital. On the way from the Mortuary to the Church, he was greatly moved by peoples reactions on the street. As the hearse passed by, practically everyone blessed themselves. To think that complete strangers had so much respect for his gran, someone they would never know, really eased the pain on this very sad occasion.

This presented a problem for his granda who had to live alone. At his age, he was into his eighties, he was incapable of looking after himself. He approached his mother to try and persuade her to return to Donnycarney with the family. His father, still struggling to regain full health, was reluctant to move to what he perceived as a potential awkward situation. Two women in the one house rarely works, the same applies to men, and he could foresee difficulties.

But his mother was adamant, she preferred Donnycarney, the new housing estate held little in the way of anything as far as she was concerned. It made little difference to the boys, and either way, they were not consulted. There was much soul searching on the part of his father, who did not relish the thought of living under someone else's roof, but his mother was not to be denied. They were on the move again, back to where they had started from. It proved to be a strange experience for the boys, the pals they had known years before, were, like themselves 10 years older, most were working. It was odd trying to re-connect with those they had known as children. The many changes in both appearance and attitudes, it was kind of spooky being introduced to former pals who were now adults, gone were all those childish ways that they had cherished so much. It was starting all over for a second time, a period of adjustment for all of them, the one thing they all had in common was football, they could all relate to that.

It was not so simple for his father, whose fears were well founded, and at times it proved to be a fractious affair between himself and granda. The fact that granda smoked a pipe, had done all his adult life, was one reason for creating tension. He would sit by the fireplace puffing away, oblivious to his father's dislike of smoking, forcing him to leave the room in search of clean air. Over a period of time this induced resentment on his father's part, leading to exchanges between them, with his mother caught in the middle, trying to maintain a balance between the warring factions that tested her patience to the limit.

It was particularly difficult for his father during the winter months, at least he could always go outside in the fine weather. One of granda's most annoying habits was the way he had of reading the evening paper. Having read a page, he would then proceed to take the newspaper apart, page by page, leaving a jumble of paper for someone else to sort out, usually his mother. This drove his father mad having to reassemble the newspaper every evening. They even tried stapling the pages together but it was a disaster, granda simply tore the pages into strips, leaving a 'jigsaw ' of newspaper on the floor.

As always the children were oblivious to the smouldering resentment building up in their father, who probably felt that he was being pushed out of the way by his mother in favour her father. He resented not being in a position to provide for his family, at least the house in Ballyfermot had been in his name.

It came as a terrible shock to them when they learned that his father had decided to leave home and take a flat in nearby Marino. Needless to say they were not consulted or asked for an opinion. It left the boys devastated, it was unthinkable that their father would feel the need to leave home without discussing it with them. They were so involved in their own little worlds, that they were not aware of what was happening in their own home. It caused much confusion for the boys, they not being privy to what had taken place. They knew that there were some differences between their father and their granda but never thought it would ever come to this.

His mother tried to put a brave face on it, but never discussed it with them. Surely they were part of the family, if something affected one member of the family they should all be made aware of it. There was a certain stillness, a quietness about the house, like a death had taken place, and in a way it had. The loss of his father hurt him a great deal, considering all that his father had suffered over the years, it was simply not good enough for him to be treated like this. His granda did not appear to be affected by the sudden departure of his son-in-law. He continued to smoke his pipe, it being his house, he felt justified, in spite of the upset it caused to his family.

For a few weeks, to his amazement, nothing was said to try and resolve the problem, as if a veil had been drawn over the whole sad affair and forgotten. He took it upon himself to set up a meeting between his parents in a local pub, not exactly an ideal place, but something had to be done to try and resolve this stupid situation.

How do children discuss such personal matters with their parents and not appear to take sides?. They had so much respect for both of them. The meeting went on for hours, the children, hearing for the first time things they should have suspected or have been aware of, was indeed a chastening experience. It came as a great shock to learn that his father felt like a lodger. His mother denied ever acting in that manner, and all he could do was to plead with them to find some way to overcome the problem and get the family together again. Eventually it was agreed that his father would return home, on condition that granda refrain from smoking in the house whenever his father was present, mostly in the evenings.

A few days later to everyone's relief his father returned to the bosom of his family, but it was an uneasy peace. It never boiled over into open confrontation, but the air was at times tense, with both sides trying their best to avoid another breakdown. To try and apportion blame was not easy; his mother probably should have been more sensitive to their father's needs, especially after his long illness. Likewise, his father could have been a little more tolerant towards others. As for granda, what can one say, he was an old man, set in his ways, change does not come easy.

Things were never quite the same again. That openness, that easy way was gone. A further deterioration in his father's health a number of years later, resulted in a return to the weekly visits to another sanatorium, this time in Blanchardstown. He would remember to his dying days, that last Christmas, when his father had been let home for the festive season, and how he had pleaded with them to be allowed return to the hospital, where he felt safe. It ended with him dying, a slow, painful death from cancer, in 1969 after so many years of isolation from his family.

With Jackie Bennett on the Eiffel Tower 1957.

CHAPTER 19

Continental Holidays.

'DID you ever see anything like it in all your life?' asked a disappointed Sean. 'The ref must be blind'.

'Your man, Kirby was at least two yards offside when he scored that last goal,' replied a scornful Owen.

'Is that the same ref who put us out of the cup last year?' inquired Jackie.' He's a complete wagon'.

A group of them were coming home from a football match in Tolka Park where they had just witnessed the defeat of their team, Drumcondra by their arch rivals, Shamrock Rovers. To say they were not impressed, would be putting it mildly, having waited weeks for the fixture, it was heartbreaking to come away, knowing that no matter how much they complained, nothing was going to change the result.

'Forget the match, here's something more important', said the ever resourceful Owen, as they stopped beside the park, to talk about, what else, but football. 'I got this out of the paper yesterday, it's about an Aer Lingus offer to France, anyone interested?'.

'What do you mean, forget about football!' stated Peter, a football fanatic. 'What else is there?'.

'You can fly to France for as little as thirteen pounds', answered Owen firmly.

'You must be joking, it costs three times that to fly to London,' came the quick reply.

'See for yourselves, that's what it says here,' insisted Owen, handing the newspaper cutting around. 'What do you'se think?'.

'What are you suggesting?' asked a surprised Brian, not to sure what Owen was talking about.

'A continental holiday', replied Owen with conviction.

'You must be kidding', answered Sean, 'the furthest any of us have got is to Bray, and even that was only a day trip'.

'Where's your sense of adventure?' asked Owen passionately.' Just think of it, us strolling down the Champs d'Elysee in Paris'.

'What in the name of Jassus, would the likes of us be doing in Paris?' inquired the sceptical Peter.

'If you have to ask a stupid question like that, I feel sorry for you'. responded Owen, shaking his head. 'We'll never get a better opportunity to see the most beautiful city in the world'.

'Are you sure it's the city you want to see?' asked Brian,' and not something else?

'What are you suggesting?' asked Owen, 'what else is there in Paris to see?'.

'The cost would be out of our price range', interjected the quiet Jackie. 'Still, I know a girl, Maureen Cronin who works in Hewett's the travel agents, she might be able to give us an idea of the cost involved'.

'Great, first how many are interested?' asked Owen, getting excited at the prospect of a trip to France. 'The offer only lasts a few weeks, the sooner we know the better'.

'It's back to our parents again,' Peter answered, not enamoured with the thought of having to ask his parents. 'In the end, it will be them, not us, who decide'.

Soundings were taken, and naturally it caused a few waves, especially with the mothers. The thought of their darling sons, heading for the perceived 'flesh pots' of Paris did not sit to well with some of them, but mostly the reaction was favourable. Perhaps the parents, who had come through a long period of hard times, even welcomed the notion. Something that they could never have aspired to, even dreamed about, a sign that life was on the up at last.

In the meantime, Jackie made the necessary inquiries and came up with an itinerary that included, trains, and bed and breakfast accommodation. His conclusion was that, if each of them saved a pound a week between now and August, plus three weeks holiday pay, they would have enough to cover expenses, with a few bob over for spending money. After each of them had discussed the proposed trip with their respective parents, the word came back that some of parents expressed a view that as part of the holiday, that they should consider making a trip to Lourdes. This was not well received by the majority of the gang. Apart from the cost, which would have been considerable, a religious shrine held no great interest for them. They had more than enough religion at home, to last them a lifetime!

Finally, after much soul searching and a lot of talking, a party of six paid their deposit, the deal was struck. It was then a case of, save, save, save, every penny counted. There was also the not inconsiderable matter of passports to be acquired, the filling in of an endless number of forms, the search for birth certificates. This was followed by photographs, travellers cheques, and French currency, that came in handfuls. As the fateful day drew ever so close, all kinds of suggestions were made by well meaning friends, who had been no further than Holyhead and had never set foot on the mainland of Europe. They knew nobody who been across the English channel, and as for an aeroplane, the same applied.

Each on them were in a state of high excitement as they boarded the bus for the Dublin airport, waving goodbye to family and friends, as they set off on the great adventure. The usual confusion at the airport, waiting to board, tickets at the ready, the long walk to the plane, until they were finally seated, airborne and heading for France, in a very noisy propeller driven plane. The flight was smooth and quick, the only glitch was the food served on flight, it did nothing to satisfy their hunger. The plane landed with a slight bump in Cherbourg, much to their relief. After the almost ceremonial checking of passports by stern faced officials, they were directed by hand signals to the railway station. At least they hoped so! The journey to Paris was a pleasant trip through green countryside, very much like that at home, except the houses were completely different. Their first sight of Paris as it came into view, filled them with excitement. They were actually in Paris, a bunch of nobodies, from Dublin! The train came to halt in Gare St. Lazare and they tumbled out on to a crowded platform, dragging their suit cases behind them, surrounded by signs pointing in every direction, in French, of course. Naturally, they had to wait while Owen went in search of a toilet. Eventually he returned, looking a little grey around the gills.

'Owen, are you all right?' inquired Jackie. 'You look like you have just seen a ghost'.

'You can say that again,' retorted a somewhat distressed Owen, 'you should see what they call the 'Jacks'.

'What are you talking about?' replied Brian, 'who may I ask, wants to know about toilets?'

'But this one has no pan, just a hole in the floor,' replied an appalled Owen, shaking his head in disbelief.

'You're not serious?' answered Jackie, clearly as shocked at what he had heard.

'Sure as God made little apples', said Owen, as he crossed his heart. 'It's unbelievable'.

They came out of the station, still discussing the merits or otherwise of the toilets, on to the Rue d'Amsterdam in search of the Hotel Deauville, which has had booked into. Half way up the street, they found it, a small, comfortable looking hotel, perfect for their needs. The next move was to be a little awkward, as they could not speak a word of French and as they soon found out, the consierge at the reception could not speak English. Then there followed a great deal of pointing and the waving of hands, before they were eventually shown to their rooms on the second floor, first having to lodge their passports with the concierge. Two fine, bright rooms with three beds in each room. It was quickly decided who was to share the rooms. They really were in Paris!

After unpacking and washing, they went for a stroll, just to get the feel of the place. One of the first things that struck them was the noise and speed of the traffic. Every car would tear up to the traffic lights, followed by the screeching of brakes if the lights changed to red, causing them to fear for their own safety. The streets were full of people taking the evening air and smoking the most obnoxious, evil smelling cigarettes imaginable called 'Gauloise'. Passing the many bars, crowded with customers drinking coffee and other forms of refreshments. They would have liked to venture in but the 'language' barrier prevented them. In fact, they were too scared to even try. About an hour later they returned to the hotel, to be greeted by a smiling consierge, who handed them the keys of their respective rooms. It had been an eventful day for each of them, the tiredness had got to them, and sleep came easy.

Next morning, they were awakened by the noisy traffic that roared up and down the street outside but mostly the screeching of brakes.

'An early start, we have a lot to see,' said Jackie. As they made their way to the reception, where the concierge had coffee and croissants layed out for them.

'Jassus, that's the best coffee I have ever tasted', said Owen, as he gulped down his second cup. 'A far cry from that dreadful 'Irel' coffee we're forced to drink at home.

The croissants were quickly put to death, which none of them had ever seen, never mind tasted them before, and all agreed, that they were hooked.

'First stop, the Eiffel Tower,' announced Owen, and for once there was no dissenting voice.

The only way to see Paris, is by the 'Metro' and the least expensive way to do that, is to get a weekly ticket, but who would be brave enough to approach the ticket desk without a word of French between them. They had a phrase book, not that it was much use, as they could not pronounce any of the words.

'Tell you what we can do,' said the ever patient Jackie, 'if we write down the words for a weekly ticket and show it to the ticket clerk, it might do the trick'.

'That's a brilliant idea,' replied the bold Owen,' why didn't I think of that?

'Do you really want an answer?' came the quick reply.

Owen just made a face at them.

After much searching through the phrase book, they arrived at what they thought was a reasonable proposal to be presented at the ticket desk.

'Jackie, you go first,' invited Peter, 'after all, it was your idea'.

'Thanks a lot,' answered Jackie. 'I'm sorry I ever mentioned it in the first place'.

Nevertheless, he reluctantly joined the queue for the ticket desk, with the gang in the wings to await developments. His turn came and he handed the precious note, not knowing what to expect. The desk clerk slowly examined the fateful note, he then looked at Jackie, who at this stage felt like a schoolboy handing in a sick note to his teacher, and just as scared. The clerk deliberated for a minute or so, before speaking. To Jackie, it felt like an hour, before he spoke.

'Vous voulais un billet pour le semaine, Monsieur?'

Jackie just stared, with his mouth wide open, unable to utter a word, before blurting out, 'I do not understand'.

The clerk was unmoved by the reply and answered coldly in near perfect English.' You are English?'

'No, I'm Irish'.

'Ah, that's better,' his face changed to a broad smile, 'you require a weekly ticket for the Metro?'

'Yes, and so do my friends', answered a relieved Jackie.

The clerk insisted on dealing with each of the gang in their turn, much to the annoyance of the other passengers in the queue. He had a word with each of them, before wishing them 'Bon vacances'. It was a happy and relieved gang that made their way down to the underground train, where more confusion confronted them, as they tried to understand the workings of the system. From studying the wall charts, Owen announced that it was a piece of cake.

'Simple really, each train goes from one destination to the other, with stops in between.'

'It depends on what colour line you want', interrupted Peter.' If we are on the blue line and we have to change to the green line, you pick where the intersection is and change accordingly'.

Safely on board the crowded train and hanging on to the over head straps, they arrived at their destination, the Eiffel Tower. Emerging from the dark underground into the bright sunlight, they were overpowered by the sheer size of the Tower. It reached right into the sky. The closer they got, the larger it became, till they were standing directly underneath, looking up.

'My God, how did they manage to put it together?' said Sean, expressing each of their thoughts out loud.

'I wouldn't like to have to paint that yoke,' remarked Owen, he being a house painter by trade. 'You would need danger money as well as height money on a job like that.'

'By the time you painting that, it would be time to start again'. interjected Jackie.' Come on, let's climb it'.

The tickets were purchased and with great enthusiasm they launched themselves on to the cast iron steps and commenced climbing. By the time they reached the third floor, the pace began to slacken. On reaching the top floor, they were out of breath and unable to speak for about ten minutes.

Even then, their breath came slowly, and it was some time before they could really appreciate the stunning view, Paris lay at their feet.

'Jassus, did you ever see anything like it in your life?' asked Owen on regaining his speech.

It was fantastic, for miles they could see in every direction. They just stood there gazing without saying a word. Words could not describe the scene below. Six poor Dublin slobs, perched on the Eiffel Tower, in the centre of Paris, enjoying one of the most spectacular and uplifting views in the world.

'And we thought Nelson's Pillar was high,' said Jackie with a dry smile. 'Compared with this, it is more like a glorified matchstick'.

As they were about to leave, he bent down and picked up a piece of paper off the ground.

'That's a bit of luck,' said Peter, holding up a brand new English pound note.

'It's true what they say, the devil looks after his own,' stated Brian, shaking his head.

'As the old lady said when she pissed in the sea, every little helps,' answered Brian with a big smile.

'You know what, your gorgeous,' replied Brian.

'Jealousy will get you nowhere', came the response from Peter. 'The only difference is, that I saw it first'.

Down the long steps to the ground floor, still in awe of the huge structure they had just climbed.

'Hey, there's an old fella over there selling fruit, lets try some'. invited Owen., referring to a street trader standing beside a hand drawn barrow that was laden down with a variety of exotic fruit, some of which they had never seen or tasted before.

'Those peaches look good,' said Brian, who for once, much to everyone's surprise took the lead and purchased a bag full of peaches. He was a rather nervous type, not much given to acts of bravery. The peaches were almost twice the size of peaches back home and less than half the price, not that they had tasted many before. Retiring to a seat in the park beside the Trocadero building, they enjoyed the sheer pleasure of 'real' peaches, and not the marbles that passed as peaches back home, stuffing themselves as never before, the juice running down their faces, but who cared, this was the life.

'Next stop, the Arc d'Triumphe', announced Peter, who was also coming out of his shell and beginning to assert himself. Straight down the Avenue Kleber, they could see the Arch in the distance.

The long walk through the crowed street really opened their eyes to what style really meant. The elegant dress of both women and men, made them feel like refugees from a third world country, which they probably were, at that time. As for the shops, just looking at the window displays, was telling them that they had a lot of ground to make up before their standard of living came within an ass's roar of France. Considering that France had suffered during the war, while Ireland had been spared the worst horrors of that same war the difference was striking.

Like the Eiffel Tower, the Arc was a splendid monument, situated at an intersection where as many as twelve roads converged. The problem was, how to cross the road through the fast moving traffic without loss of life or limb, where every car seemed to practicing for grand prix race. Carefully observing how the locals managed to make their way to the centre, Owen had the bright idea of walking beside an old lady as she crossed, thus giving them some protection from the mad car drivers. It was with relief that they finally made it to the centre, but not without some hair raising experiences. The fact that traffic was also on the 'wrong' side of the road did not help either. They tagged on to a group of tourists, that turned out to be English, with a guide explaining the significance and historical importance of the Arc.

'Tell you what,' said Brian, 'I don't know about you'se, but I'm starving,

I'm so hungry that I could eat a farmer's arse through a thorn hedge'.

'So would I,' replied Owen.

'No sign of a 'chipper' round here, that's for sure,' answered Peter.

'Where are we going to find a restaurant that we can afford?' asked Sean seriously.

'We passed a tourist office just back there,' said Jackie, 'they'd be sure to know of a reasonable place to eat'.

Retracing their steps, they entered the office and one again Jackie was obliged to do the needful, while the rest of them pretended to admire the many picturesque posters on display.

He came back with an armful of literature, detailing every place to eat, including prices. A search through them turned up just the place they were looking for, a self-service restaurant. The prospect of going to a normal restaurant was too daunting. Not knowing the language or the cost was more than they were capable of, it was back to the Metro.

It took some time and persistence before they found what they were looking for, and it was worth all the trouble. They were able to choose for themselves from a fine display of food, at a price that suited their pocket. It was to serve them well that week. After enjoying a good meal, it was postcard time. A selection of them were purchased, including stamps, for family and friends. Back to the hotel, weary from their travels, tired feet were washed in the foot bath, or so they thought. (It was years before they discovered, that in fact, it was 'Bidet'.)

The following morning they were again treated to a breakfast of coffee and criossants plus marmalade to spread on them. The perfect start to the day. Out on to the street, as fresh as a daisy with a jaunt in their step, they were coming out of their world. Away from the constraints of their parents, six young men on the verge of life, without a care in the world.

'What's on for today?' inquired Brian.

'Why not Notre Dame,' replied Peter, 'I hear it is an amazing place'.

'Notre Dame it is'

Coming up out of the underground, they had their first sight of the cathedral. It's dark, mysterious appearance conjured up visions of 'Quasimodo' the Hunchback clinging from the battlements with bells ringing loudly. On entering, they blessed themselves with holy water and walked into the dark and eerie cavern that was the cathedral. They were a little surprised at how dark and cold it was, quite unlike any church back home. A mixture of candle smoke and incense filled the place, that was crowded with people, just rambling about, ignoring the fact that they were in the house of God. They spoke in whispers, as was the normal practice. Not everyone observed the silence, with people chatting away as if they were on the street. The interior was dominated by a magnificent circular stained glass window about forty feet in diameter, with the bright sun light illuminating it's glorious colours. There was really not that much to see but before leaving, they knelt and said a few prayers.

'I didn't think much of that place,' said a disappointed Brian when they were outside. 'It was kind of creepy'.

'Spooky, might be better way of describing it,' replied Sean, 'didn't feel like cathedral to me, in fact it gave me the creeps'.

'Peaches, more peaches,' cried Owen who has been greatly taken by them.

'If I were you, I'd be careful eating too much fruit,' warned Jackie, 'you could get the run'.

'I don't care, it would be worth it,' replied the ever cheerful Owen, searching the street for one of the street traders'

'Remember what the toilets are like here,' reminded Brian. This brought a knowing frown to Owen's face'

'Speaking about toilets,' said Sean,' look at your man over there, on the side of the street.' Pointing at a metal structure that housed a public urinal stall.

'Oh my God,' replied a shocked Owen,' your man over there is using the 'jacks', with his feet and head sticking out'.

'What harm is it?' asked Jackie. 'It's a normal bodily function'.

'We understand that but at the side of the street, with everyone watching? Ah, come on', responded a disgusted Owen.

By the end of the week, they somehow managed to over come their dislike of the public utility, and were quite content to make use of it, but at the same time, keeping their heads down.

They headed for the 'Louvre,' the most famous Art Gallery in the world, only to find a queue, and it took ages before they finally managed to gain entrance. A ticket purchased at a nominal rate enabled them to view part of the gallery but it turned out to be a false charge. For each section of the gallery, an extra fee was required, which when added up it amounted to more than they were prepared to pay. By the time they reached the section that contained the famous 'Mona Lisa' they had had enough. Even though it was the principle attraction, they turned away and left, disappointed but determined not to be taken for a ride.

'Not to worry,' said Sean, as they turned away in the direction of the Champs Elysee,' maybe next time'.

'You must be joking' answered Owen firmly! We only wanted to see the bloody picture, not buy it'.

After the disappointment of the Louvre, the long walk down the

Champs Elysee made them feel better.

The tree lined boulevard certainly opened their eyes to what a high class place it was. The shops displayed the most expensive clothes imaginable, with a single shirt costing more than a months pay. A real eye opener. One thing that never failed to arouse their attention, was, that both men and women wore 'perfume', or the equivalent. This was before they had heard of deodorant or after shave. At home you would be looked upon as a little odd, even a sissy for wearing 'perfume'.

They had an early evening but not before Brian drew their attention to something rather strange in the hotel

'I'm telling you, it rings,' said Brian emphatically. 'If you don't believe me, try for yourself'.

Three of them were sitting in their room having an argument about, of all things, the hotel stairs.

'Your dreaming,' insisted Sean.' Things like that only happen in the pictures'.

'Go and see for yourself,' snapped Brian, annoyed that they would not take him seriously.

To settle the argument, Jackie volunteered to go down the stars, out on to the street and return immediately.

'Just listen and you'll believe me,' insisted Brian, 'perhaps you'd like to have a small wager?'

'Knock it off you two,' interrupted Jackie. 'I'll be back in a minute.' Away he went, and sure enough, when he returned he confirmed, that indeed the 4th step of the stairs, when tread upon, triggered off a bell in the office of the concierge, who appeared like magic at the desk, to wish one and all 'Bonjour'.

'That's the craziest thing I have ever heard,' cried Sean, surprised at what had just been revealed. 'What's all that in aid of?'

'It's obvious,' answered Brian, happy that he had been vindicated. 'Your man is at the desk in case someone tries to do a bunk without paying'.

'Jassus, if that doesn't beat Banagher, nothing does,' replied Sean, shaking his head in disbelieve.' All that just to save a few bob'.

'He must have got stung a few times to go through all that trouble,' said Jackie, just as surprised as the others.

Over the next few days they continued their voyage of discovery, visiting every single place mentioned in the guide book, with the exception of Pigalle and Versaille, much to the annoyance of Owen, who regularly offered to go on his own to Pigalle, just to see what it 'looked like'. Each time he mentioned Pigalle, the response he got was negative. The warnings they had received from their parents, included that particular part of the city. Not the sort of place a good Catholic boy would go near.

'We'll leave Versaille till the day before we go home,' suggested Jackie, who had become, a sort of unofficial leader of the gang.' Save the best for last'.

One aspect of Parisian life that fascinated them was the number of coloured and Oriental people they encountered on the street. Never, ever having seen or spoken to a person other than white, they could not help themselves staring. If the other person returned the stare, they could only drop their eyes with embarrassment. For them it was a completely new experience, especially the Oriental's. They all seemed so small and petite. The only Oriental's they had ever seen, had been in an old 'Charlie Chan'. picture.

The journey to Versaille by train was uneventful and they arrived at around midday. They were a little surprised to find themselves virtually alone on the station with not a soul in sight, except the porter. Following the well posted signs, they set off in the direction of the beautiful chateau, something they had looked forward to seeing. Their final place of interest. The magnificent gates of the chateau came into sight, but to their amazement, they were closed, locked, no entrance. Deflated, they could not ask anyone. Even if they did meet someone, what was the point, unless that person spoke English. It was back to the station, the journey had been a complete waste of time and money.

'Ask your man over there,' suggested Brian, pointing at the railway porter'

'Ask him what?' replied Jackie.' In case you haven't noticed, I don't speak French'.

'Maybe he speaks a little English,' insisted Brian, at the same time, he was distancing himself from having to approach the Porter. To Jackie's credit, reluctantly he went, phrase book at the ready and 'spoke' to the porter, as best as he could. The porter, for his part, listened carefully, waving his arms, shrugged his shoulders. He muttered something to Jackie, who thanked him for his assistance.

'It seems that the chateau is closed one day a week,' said Jackie to his waiting audience, 'and guess what day that is?'

'Trust us to come the only day it is not open,' cried Owen. 'Anyone would come on an opening day but not us. Oh, no, we have to miss the boat'.

'Don't blame me,' answered Jackie quickly.' I only asked the question'.

'No one is blaming you, Jackie,' insisted Sean, 'it's just our bad luck, that's all, no point in cribbing'.

'Come on, lets get back to town,' interrupted Owen. 'At least Pigalle won't be closed, it is our last chance to see it'.

After waiting for over a hour, the train finally arrived. The return journey was a quiet affair, reflecting the fact that the holiday was nearing it's inevitable conclusion. No one said very much. It had been a wonderful experience, far beyond their wildest dreams, now it was about to finish, and it was time for reflection.

'This is the last throw of the dice,' announced Owen, ever pushing his case to visit either the 'Follies Bergere' or the 'Moulin Rouge', much to the discomfort of the others. 'What do you'se say, our last day in Paris, we make tracks for Pigalle?'

'I don't know, you hear so many stories about that place,' said Brian. Secretly he too wanted to see for himself, more out of curiosity than anything else.

'Ah, for Jassus sake', answered an annoyed Owen, 'we might never get another chance like this'.

Then followed a long discussion, with some wanting to go the whole hog, show and all, others were not convinced that it was proper, with the warnings from their respective parents ringing in their ears. Their parents had trusted them and they had no desire to break that trust.

'Tell you what', said the ever sensible Jackie, trying to avoid a split in the camp, 'say we go and take a look, then we can decide what to do.'

It was agreed.

So that evening, all dressed in their best clobber, hair slicked back with 'Brylcreem', they set off to visit the notorious red light district of Paris. To say they were in any way brave, would be an overstatement. In fact they were scared stiff at the prospect of what they might encounter. Having heard so many stories, they were extremely nervous. They located the brightly lit 'Moulin Rouge' and stood across the street for a long time, trying to decide, what to do.

'I'm going to get a closer look', said the ever resourceful Owen, and with that he crossed to the other side of the crowded street, leaving them to ponder their fate. Eventually he was joined by the others, a little shamed faced, as he admired the many pictures on display, of 'ladies' in various stages of undressing. The Commissioner all done up in a fancy uniform, with a peaked cap, urging all comers to come and see the show. It proved to be more than they had bargained for, even the redoubtable Owen, for once, he was at a loss for words.

'What do you say?' said Brian, breaking the awkward silence.' Lets go and have a meal, in a proper restaurant for a change. It someone asks when we get home, at least we can brag that we went to the 'Moulin Rouge' even if it was only for meal'.

'Have we enough money?' inquired Sean: 'Some of these places will take you to the cleaners. Look at the prices on the menu, they look kind of expensive to me'.

'Your right, I don't want to spend my last day in Paris washing dishes'. answered Jackie.

They counted the money they had between them and decided to take a chance.

They were ushered to a table by a typical French waiter, complete with a tiny moustache. After a discussion with the waiter, who mercifully spoke English, they were served a fine meal. After the main course, they were served a lovely pie, cut in sections, which they presumed was dessert, only to discover to their horror, that it was a strong 'Camembert' cheese that nearly poisoned them. Cheese was not a normal part of their diet at home. The only cheese they ever tasted was a mild cheese and the name Camembert meant nothing to them. The meal finished and it was back to the hotel, to prepare for tomorrow's departure.

With a final farewell to the concierge they headed for the railway station and home, to be greeted by family and friends on their arrival in Dublin airport. It was to be the first of many such holidays in Europe, but somehow, that first, tentative step into the great big world out there, remained fixed in their minds forever. It certainly opened their eyes to a world, so far removed from anything they or their parents had ever experienced or imagined.

SLANG WORDS OR EXPRESSIONS*